For Amalia

so much love
Mixed with sadness and joy—

Joanie

Another Kind of Time

Published by aah-ha! Books, Inc.
http://www.starwater.com

For information address: aah-ha! Books, Inc.
12 Virginia Court, Amityville, NY 11701
(516) 598-8842

aah-ha! Books are published by aah-ha! Inc.
Its trademark, consisting of the words aah-ha! Books and logo,
is registered in U.S. Patent and Trademark Office
Library of Congress Catalog Card #98-88825

ISBN 1-889853-55-0

PRINTED IN HONG KONG

0 2 4 6 8 9 7 5 3 1

Another Kind of Time

Joan B. Brady

For Mummy with Love

During the past four years

there have been many wise and generous people

who have taken the time to encourage and guide me

throughout the making of this book.

To you always...my gratitude and love.

"Be with those who help your being.

Don't sit with indifferent people, whose breath

Comes cold out of their mouths.

Not these visible forms, your work is deeper.

A chunk of dirt thrown in the air breaks to pieces.

If you don't try to fly,

And so break yourself apart,

You will be broken open by death,

When it's too late for all you could become."

~Rumi:

"Rumi...These Branching Moments"

Translated by John Moyne & Coleman Barks

To My Beloved Midwives:

Chris Bamford
Susan M.S. Browne
Bob Brothers
Rhonda deJong
Carol Gino
Will Marsh

Who, with their caring hearts and professional hands,
have helped me birth my book into it's physical form.

INTRODUCTION

When I was a little girl, there were things I "knew"...and then forgot...and know again now.

I knew that life was like a great, big secret...and every year that you got older...and wiser...you would be allowed to know a little bit more. I knew, also, that I could speak directly to God.

Most of my youth was spent daydreaming and dancing and falling in love with love. I was a terrible student, except in math and art and philosophy. I still remember loving to play out the stories of the Greek gods and goddesses with two friends on weekends in the fifth grade! Mostly, I think I was just asleep.

"Our birth is but a sleep and a forgetting,
The soul that rises within us, our life's star,
Hath had elsewhere its setting,
And cometh from afar.
Not in entire forgetfulness
But trailing clouds of glory do we come
From God who is our home."

~William Wordsworth

In my twenties, I fell in love with my husband, Jimmy, got married, and had three beautiful babies. I thought that that was all I was meant to do. My life felt as though it had finally clicked in.

In my thirties I had fun, up to my ears in kids' activities, their schools, the community, sports, and social events, and began to find out what I could do. I also began painting watercolors.

At forty, my world as I knew it began to fall apart, and I began asking the questions...

"Who am I...and what am I doing here...really?"

Remember the song that Peggy Lee sang..."Is that all there is?"

Alone in my studio, I plunged into painting and began to dig deeper. I began experimenting with meditation and its effects on my painting. Amazing. If I didn't spend time "sitting" before I began painting, I found that I would paint "ditzy", all over the surface, just like my head...but, if I took twenty to thirty minutes to calm and empty my mind beforehand, then I could go immediately into a deep place to paint from, where my head was no longer involved, and, from where surprising things would often happen. Sometimes, I felt as though I hadn't even done the painting myself.

Searching...looking beyond, looking deep...for the source of all creativity. A gentle yearning...a knowing from somewhere else...exploded into a passion for learning about the hidden things of the soul. Certainly, this was not from school, where I never did the reading, the homework.

Books began to find me, jumping into my hands in bookstores, coming from the most surprising places and people. The bookshelves and tabletops began to fill with books on mysticism, astrology, alternative medicine, philosophy, psychology, metaphysics, Buddhism, Vedanta, as I devoured two and three at a time.

For a number of years, I knew of no one in our circle of family and friends to share my passion with. Instead, my heavy-handed attempts to plunge into these subjects was too often met with disdain and distaste, a rolling of the eyes, if not outright hostility.

"Mind has mattered so much, and knowledge
Is bottomless as the golden bowl
In the myth, ceaseless as light, Grave
Unemptiable as the sea…
To know, to understand
Has been my passion and addiction."

~Barbara Howes (obituary New York Times, Feb '96)

But help began to come…first with books and tapes…then, a few years later, with a friend…and another friend…and eventually an increasing number of like minded spirits.

For the past twenty five years, I've been on a mystical treasure hunt, feeling like a dog with a bone…not knowing if I'm the dog or the bone…searching to understand increasingly the reasons for my being here…to remember what I knew when I arrived here, and then forgot. Once you've opened the inner door, the "Hound of Heaven" won't leave you alone.

What began as a little flame of understanding, then turned into a bonfire fed by pain and joy, has now subsided into an eternal smoldering which fills me alternately with laughter, tears, and awe...a knowing and longing for Home.

Attempting to live as a contemplative in an active life, an artist between events, a mystic in a privileged world, is truly a balancing act. Losing track of time in the midst of doing what I love most reminds me...to remember.

Arranging flowers, painting, gardening, preparing a meal and setting the table for friends, connecting with people...all these things intertwine in one act of gratitude, one lifelong meditation.

"Deep thinking emerges from our own patch of ground, our own garden, from simple seeds...never abstract...intensely practical because it is a personal practice, a way of self-reliance, such as growing one's own vegetables."

~Lex Hixon

My mother believed in fairies.
When my younger sister Kate and I were
little, Mummy used to lead us deep into
the woods near our house to see where
the fairies lived...to places where the moss
grew all velvety and soft, over stumps and
rocks...to dark crevices and crannies in tree trunks
and branches where she told us they slept and ate
and went to school. I believed it then and
I believe it still.
I glimpse their wings in my garden now
and then and feel their presence here and
there...especially when I'm not really looking.

BEFORE

From the few photographs and even fewer memories that Mummy shared with us about her own childhood, she must have been a beautiful little girl. Katherine Roe Slade had big, brown, expressive eyes, naturally curly auburn hair, and dimples in both cheeks.

Her father, Prescott Slade, died in 1912, when she was four. She had no memories of him at all. Her mother, Josephine, who never remarried, then moved with her son, Roe, and her daughter into her own parents' house in Highland Falls, New York, on the Hudson River. At the time, Mummy's maternal grandfather, Charles Francis Roe, was a major general in the United States Army at nearby West Point Academy.

Years before, as a young lieutenant and commanding officer of Company F of the Second Cavalry, Roe had led his battalion of soldiers to join his commanding officer, Gen. George Custer of the Seventh Cavalry, to fight what turned out to be thousands of Sioux and Cheyenne Indians at the Battle of the Little Big Horn in southeastern Montana. As his later accounts state, the night of June 27, 1876, was as "dark as a pocket," and his company got lost several times on the way.

Either Roe was late or General Custer jumped the gun, but when he arrived at the appointed place, he looked down at the plains of the Little Big Horn and witnessed the horrible aftermath of the now famous battle. The next morning, he wrote a note hastily in pencil to "My Darling Wife" describing what he had seen there. "The battle field is simply horrible. Two hundred and four soldiers' and officers' bodies in one place. The whole valley for two miles is dead horses and soldiers."

Mummy adored the man she called "Grampy." His portrait shows a tall man with a kind face, partially covered by a golden mustache and beard and a pair of pincenez glasses on the bridge of his nose. He stands proudly in his uniform, his chest covered with medals.

Mummy was the apple of his eye. One of her earliest memories was riding horseback at his side along the banks of the Hudson River, leaving calling cards at friends' houses along the way. She was a rebellious and free-spirited little girl, and this was not something she particularly liked to do. But in that puritanical and patriarchal world, she was brought up to behave herself in front of grown-ups.

I remember a photograph of Mummy as a girl of twelve, sitting on the steps of a log cabin next to a Crow Indian, a scout named Curley, who had witnessed the Battle of the Little Big Horn. It was taken when her grandfather traveled west in 1920 to make his own peace with the people he had fought against forty-four years before.

Mummy always said of her childhood that she got too much attention. Her best friend growing up was the family cook's daughter, whose father once told her she was a spoiled brat. She never forgot it.

I think she also felt guilty later that she had led such a privileged and seemingly easy life compared with that of her brother, Roe, whose youth was marred by mastoid operations and a growing dependency on alcohol.

He left Yale before he graduated and married Marie Bonnard, a young Frenchwoman who had been hired some years before as a governess for him and Mummy. They never had any children.

Around 1920 my grandmother moved with her two children to New York City and put them in private schools there. Mummy was sent to "Miss Brearley's." From there, she went away to boarding school at "Miss Walker's" in Connecticut, where she made many friends. The finishing touch to her education was a year in Paris, where she lived with a French family and attended La Sorbonne.

She adored dancing and was a natural actress. Her expressions were mischievous, flirty, fiery, and kind. She had a caught-at-something look, a dreamy, faraway gaze, and a wide open and warm-as-could-be smile that dazzled everyone.

Mummy was tall, five foot six and a half, with beautiful, long and shapely legs. She had pretty hands with long, artistic fingers. And she had the softest skin. She was naive yet savvy, naughty yet dignified, and for a while was a real flapper. She had tons of beaux and dancing partners, some of whom were in love with her and all of whom loved her spontaneity and charm.

But Daddy was the one she chose. Henry Babcock, who had also grown up in New York City, was bright and handsome and very funny. He was over six feet tall and had dark brown hair that looked shiny and black. He wore round silver-rimmed glasses over his very blue eyes. He was a beautiful dancer, and, together, they made quite a pair.

They got married on December 19, 1930. After living in a couple of short-term rental houses, they bought their first home, a two-story, whitewashed brick house on Berry Hill Road in Syosset, Long Island. Four years later, I was born, and two and a half years after that, my sister Kate arrived. Henry Junior joined us in 1940. He had Mummy's brown eyes. She used to push him sometimes, bundled up and covered by a fur throw, in his English carriage to the village to show him off. Our family lived in this house, which we children called "Sunshine House," for twelve or thirteen years.

Mummy loved fresh air, and there were always long weekend walks with my parents and one or two springer spaniels across cornfields, through woods, and by ponds with giant cat-o'-nine-tails. Mummy loved her children and joined right in with whatever we were doing. Playing games came most naturally to her. For days, she patiently tried to teach me to ride a bicycle. I remember falling and falling...and then throwing the bike down in a furor. I still have blue scars on my knees from the gravel driveway. She'd help me pick it up, and somehow was able to make it all fun, even when it hurt.

Mummy traveled with us through so many children's books, enchanted by the pictures, caught up by the dramas.... *Beccasine and Madeline, Babar and Celeste,* "*The Wind in the Willows,*" "*Winnie the Pooh,*" "*The Little Prince,*" "*The Peterkin Papers,*" "*Grimms' Fairy Tales*", "*The Bobbsey Twins,*" and the "*The Snow Goose.*" She made them so real that, for years, I had a dream about Colin and Mary in "*The Secret Garden*" that I could recall at will when I woke up.

And, most vivid of memories, we kept returning to the woods, with and without Mummy, to visit the places where the fairies lived and danced.

Mummy was always there then. She soothed my feelings of rejection when, in the nursery school circus at Miss Stoddard's School for Very Little People, I longed to be a "Flying Girl" on the swing with a beautiful ballerina costume but was told I was to be instead the rear end of a horse. Mummy truly empathized with all our childish predicaments and heartbreaks.

Daddy was there every day also, but always on his punctual schedule. He worked for most of his adult life on Wall Street as an odd lot broker. He loved it, saying it was like a giant poker game. He commuted on the Long Island Railroad, reading two newspapers on the way in and two on the way out, when he wasn't playing a game of bridge.

I remember the Christmas Eves of those early years. We drove to St. John's of Cold Spring Harbor for the evening service. I loved it when it was snowing, although Daddy grumbled a lot. But Mummy always saw the magic. The live Christmas pageant was so beautiful, so real. Except for the Nativity scene, the Easter bunny, and a little bit of Sunday School, we didn't have a whole lot of religious training. In fact, the only rituals that I remember on a regular basis growing up had to do with a silver martini shaker, which reverently appeared at exactly the same time every evening, sometimes twice a day on special occasions.

About once a week, while we lived in Syosset, we would drive about half an hour to Mill Neck to visit our grandmother, Mummy's "Muddy," Jojo to all of us. For Mummy, Jojo was a source of strength, her mentor, her best friend. Jojo had arthritis, which later crippled her so badly that she was eventually bedridden. People came to see her to cheer her up, and she always ended up hearing their stories, making them feel better and making them laugh. I used to think she was the bravest person I'd ever known, and I remember praying that if I was ever sick or in pain, I'd have her courage. The great inner strength behind her sense of humor was certainly passed down to Mummy when she needed it in her own life.

Jojo had built a large and beautiful house in 1929. (She must not have paid too much attention to the financial section of the newspaper.) Coming up the long, curved driveway and into the courtyard, we parked facing the front door at the center of the big white house with its gray slate mansard roof. Diamond-shaped windowpanes crisscrossed the double dormers along the second story and the French doors along the ground floor.

Once the ignition was turned off, all the car doors would fly open at once and we'd run into the big living room on the south end of the house, where Jojo would be sitting in a chair, waiting for us before her midday martini. After about half an hour of catching up on everyone's news, Jojo's nurse, Mary Foley, would move her into her wheelchair and we'd all follow her to the big dining room at the north end of the house.

We loved this room because the walls were covered in canvas that had been painted by an artist named Schreyvogel from prints of old West Point. There were soldiers, marching bands, women in long, bustled skirts and bonnets, children playing with balls and hoops and dogs. Boats floated on the Hudson River, which appeared and reappeared as it curved its way through the soft blue and green and maize hills and fields. In one corner, a large red brick house was tucked into the scenery. It was the house that Major General Roe and his family had lived in.

In 1945, when I was ten, we moved into Jojo's house in Mill Neck. She spent most of her time now in her apartment in New York City, occasionally, and for just a few years, coming to stay with us in what always remained her room, or renting a small place in the country nearby in the summer. Mummy never changed many of the paint colors and wallpapers that Jojo had chosen when she "created" the house. Until her death at the age of seventy-seven, Jojo remained a strong influence and inspiration in her daughter's life.

On May 15, 1945, Susie was born. No one else in my fifth grade class had a mother who produced a baby sister for them. I can still remember the next day at school, standing near the jungle gym during recess, all of my female classmates surrounding me and breaking into a cheer: "Two...four...six...eight...who do we appreciate?...Mrs. Babcock...Mrs. Babcock...Yaaaaaay!"

Daddy had a killing sense of humor. In the happy days of my youth, I can remember all of us... Daddy, Mummy, and we four children...sitting at meals around the oval-ended mahogany dining room table. He would come out with one of his one-liners, a funny twist on a mundane event, or a clever play on words. And then all of us would collapse with laughter, falling out of our chairs, tears running down our faces, usually repeating what he'd said, while he just looked surprised and pleased at what he'd caused, and, his face contorted, tried not to laugh quite as hard as we did. We were the perfect audience for him.

Christmas in Mill Neck was wonder filled, and the buildup to it was every bit as exciting. Mummy was in her element, her heart and soul involved for weeks and weeks, planning and readying just the right presents for each of the people in her life.

Mummy's off-limits "workroom" was the guest room next to her and Daddy's room. Not much light came through the deep-set double-casement dormer windows with their leaded panes. The twin poster beds and a card table were covered with mysterious boxes, bags, tissue paper, wrappings, scissors, and Scotch tape. It was a sacred space in which she made magic.

I can remember Mummy's hands, her long, lovely fingers working with the ribbon, the tags, the glitter, her reading glasses on the end of her nose. Sometimes she wore her quilted wrapper; more often she was in a pair of elastic-waisted slacks with a sweater pulled down over them. Sometimes it was quiet; sometimes the radio played Christmas music. The room had a feeling of warmth and expectancy, excitement and secrecy.

"Can I come in?"

"Just a minute…"…rustle, rustle…

"All right, just for a minute…what is it?"

That momentary peek only heightened the anticipation of what lay ahead.

On Christmas mornings, we children would wait and wait…and wait in the kitchen for what seemed like hours after we'd finished our breakfast of scrambled eggs or French toast or waffles. Then, the buzzer would ring on the house phone, signaling that Mummy and Daddy were awake, ready for their own breakfast, which would be prepared and hauled upstairs in the dumbwaiter by Georgette, our cook.

This also meant they were ready for us to come up to see if Santa Claus had stopped by and filled the stockings we had hung in their room with such care the night before. To get there, we had to circumnavigate the dining room, where the tree and the presents were waiting for us, by going up the back stairs and down the long upstairs hall.

"Merry Christmas!" we shouted as we burst through their door. There were Mummy and Daddy, sitting up in their wooden four-poster beds, breakfast trays on their laps. They looked a little sleepy but were both beaming, pleased with our delight. Mummy, particularly, looked like a radiant child who had just been given the moon. This was her real life.

Six bulging and misshapen nylon stockings were hung side by side, tacked onto the wooden mantelpiece. Round shapes, square shapes, all kind of shapes, wrapped in white tissue paper, squeezed tightly together, straining against the gossamer hosiery, in some places breaking through and causing a run or a hole.

Even after we were too old to believe anymore, we'd always burst with joy and exclaim in unison, "He came! He came!"

And then, each one of us clutching our own peculiarly shaped package, we would find a spot to sit...on the chaise lounge, at the foot of Mummy's or Daddy's bed, on the floor...and begin opening surprise after surprise, wondering out loud, "How did he know?"...whether it was Scotch tape or new mittens or bath oil or writing paper or "pretend" jewelry. Each appropriate token had been remembered and chosen carefully by Mummy, of course.

That same "How did he know?" kept me filling my own family's stockings until just a few years ago, long after my children were grown.

And Mummy and Daddy, between watching all of us and sipping their black coffee, opened their own stockings and shared private giggles over what they'd given each other, which was either useful or naughty, funny or very nice.

Later, when I was in my teens, Mummy would sometimes confide in me that she didn't really like the pin or the earrings Daddy had given her, but she didn't want to hurt his feelings. Invariably, she wore whatever it was for Christmas lunch, anyway.

By late morning, we'd be lined up outside the closed double doors to the dining room...the youngest, Susie, first; me last...until everyone had arrived. The doors were flung open to...Wow! The tree was lit up with large colored bulbs, tinsel dripped off every branch, presents were everywhere. I thought it was all breathtaking then.

Santa Claus did all the work on Christmas Eve when we were little, trimming the tree, putting out the presents, filling the stockings, until two and then three and then four of us were old enough to help. Then I remember Daddy impatiently barking at us tree trimmers with the silver tinsel, "One strand at a time!...One strand at a time!"

Mummy found us the friendliest dolls, not fancy or stiff or expensive, but floppy, squeezable, funny rag dolls, who fit right into our games as well as our lives, and who we kept for years. Many years later, when her first grandchild, our son, Jim, was born, almost everyone in the family brought a Raggedy Ann or Andy to the hospital to keep the tradition going for another generation.

One of the loveliest parts of Christmas Day was actually when it was over. We would cozy up by the fire in the fireplace in the dining room and lose ourselves in play and make-believe by the lights of the tree. Mummy was never far away.

The most constant person in our lives other than our parents was a diminutive Frenchwoman named Georgette, a superb cook from Lyons who, with her husband, Georges, and their daughter, Janine, became part of our extended family for almost twenty-five years. When not locking horns with the governess of the moment, Georgette quickly became a kind of third parent, speaking mostly in French, even though we answered in English.

Thanks to her culinary talents and Mummy's gourmet sensibilities, our house was known for its good food. All of our friends used to love to come to our house for dinner. The more they ate, the more was offered.

Mummy rejoiced in orchestrating combinations of food that would please all the senses. Some of her favorite dishes were osso buco, rare roast beef and Yorkshire pudding, ratatouille, Georgette's special coleslaw, for which Mummy often shredded the cabbage, fresh and frenched green beans almondine, homegrown sorrel soup, mâche, known then as "field salad," braised leeks, celery, or endive, all kinds of queer vegetables. At some point during every meal, Mummy would ask for a "pusher," a piece of bread or a cracker to scoop up and soak up every last mouthful. Favorite desserts were crême brulee, crême caramel, and charlotte prièure.

Anyone who ever worked for my parents...and there were many over the years...loved them both. They were kind; they were unaffected. Mummy was the one they knew most intimately. She became involved with their lives, their children, their problems. They called her a real lady. She never did anything particularly heroic or showy. She simply was there. She was reachable, not egotistical. She lightened their lives and their loads, and she cared deeply about each one of them.

When I was young, my friends always told me that they wished my mother was their mother. They told me that I was so lucky. Of course, at the time, I couldn't see why. I saw their mothers as more glamorous, more intelligent, more "with it," or more important. Mummy was just Mummy.

By her own spontaneous actions, Mummy instilled in us a faith and a trust in the goodness of life. She had an innate sense of right and wrong. She was positive, intuitive, and warm. Full of humor and full of joy.

About the only repeated piece of advice she ever gave me, which, because of her perfect timing, irritated me beyond words, was "Joan...be yourself!"

Mummy never was anyone but herself. She never pretended; she never strove to be something other than what she was. In the busy world of doing, she was simply able to be. Her being was her doing.

And she was adorable. She was light; she was funny. Sometimes she was sad, but she hid that side of herself from most of the world that knew her.

Mummy had little secrets...with herself... and with many people, I think. She had a way of getting inside a person, first by flirting or teasing, joking and getting a rise out of them. People seemed to like it, and usually came back for more. Before they knew it, they were sharing their secrets with her.

She lived in a small and sheltered world, yet she touched a great many people, of all ages and many walks of life. Beneath the surface of the social life she led, she touched people at some deep level and they never forgot her.

She understood other people's sadnesses. She never wanted anyone, particularly her children, to be unhappy. She would suddenly look at one of us and ask, "Are you happy?" What did that question ever mean? I think she was quite psychic, so I'm sure she knew much more about all of us and our feelings than she ever told us. She often understood our secrets before we did, yet we never seemed to talk about them.

Susie always said she gave the best hugs.

Mummy loved to walk...snorting the country air, striding out with her long legs...on the beach, in the woods...with her children, her dogs, and later with her grandchildren.

I loved her flower arrangements. They looked just like her...never grand, uncontrived. Springy, alive with her spontaneous, dancing energy, brightly colored. Everything went together quite naturally. The flowers were all from her gardens....roses, peonies, iris, phlox, zinnias, yarrow, salvia, veronica...all the old-fashioned varieties mixed with sprigs of beauty bush, dogwood, apple blossoms, and forsythia.

When we couldn't find her in the house, we could almost always find Mummy in her garden, even sometimes in the rain. There she'd be on her hands and knees wearing a cotton flowered shirt, an old floppy hat pulled down over her high forehead, knee-pads strapped over her faded blue jeans, her trowel or cultivator in her right hand, rutting away at the dark brown earth, yanking out weeds, pulling off dead flower heads and stalks, her overflowing wheelbarrow attesting to the time she'd been working there. And, always, the dogs were either running around the lawn and in and out of the garden or lying in the grass by her side.

Mummy never really told us what to do and not to do. Sometimes she just blew up. Mostly she let us figure it out for ourselves.

We never, ever talked about inner things, deep feelings, about what life was all about. Mummy had her own secret cocoon of trust and safety. We were left to figure it out for ourselves.

I asked her once if she believed in God. She didn't seem too comfortable with the subject; she'd never much liked authority figures. Her faith was much more innate, beyond words. She answered that, in times of trouble, she called on her mother and asked for her help. It wasn't until many years later that I realized how important those little monthly booklets called *"Daily Word"* were in both their lives. Published by Unity, *"Daily Word"* presented a practical approach to the first-century teachings of Jesus, unhampered by theology and dogma, that gave both Mummy and Jojo strength. Mummy kept hers in a bureau drawer.

Mummy rarely went to church because, she said, she didn't like seeing the goody-goodies and the hypocrites sitting in the front row. She also worried about what she would wear if she did go.

When Mummy thought one of us had done something she didn't approve of, she didn't question us as much as give us "that look," penetrating right through to the part of you that knew you'd been pegged.

After I came home from a date or a dance with a boy, she'd usually hit me with, "What did you do with him?" Most of the time I hadn't done anything, but if I had, I certainly wouldn't have told her.

Mummy always said she was shy, that she needed that "dressing drink" to be able to go to the dinner parties that filled their evenings. She worried a lot about what other people thought or did. "Chic" people or self-important people only increased her insecurity. She was uncomfortable, "prickly" as she would say, around people who seemed to be so sure of themselves. They actually scared her.

Mummy's favorite song was "Someone to Watch over Me," and it truly expresses the way she lived her life. Her childlike trust that things would always work out, that she would be taken care of, was not only her strength but her vulnerability.

Forty-five years ago, someone sent her a thank-you note with a prayer that she showed me. Since then, it's been the first thing I've copied into my pocket diary every year. It was the overriding belief from which Mummy lived her life.

"Do not look forward to what might happen tomorrow.
The same everlasting Father, who cares for you today, will take
care of you tomorrow and every day. Either He will shield you
from suffering or He will give you unfailing strength to bear it.
Be at Peace then, and put aside all anxious thoughts and
imaginations."

~St. Francis de Sales

When I think about Mummy now, her eyes and her hands come first to my mind's eye...her long fingers meeting to hold a brush, a ribbon, a pen...a little timid, but with a mind of their own...writing letters with childlike drawings to her grandchildren, arranging flowers, tying bows, attempting to make "sailors' valentines" with shells and glue, découpaging little boxes, painting halting pictures in oil. If she ever actually finished something, it held an energy that was obviously hers. But she wasn't long on self-discipline or follow-through, so we didn't end up with many mementos.

She collected little things, curios that matched her personality, some antiques, though she didn't usually buy particularly expensive things. She loved paintings of the Hudson River School, which reminded her of her heritage and her childhood home. There, her great grandfather, Stephen Roe, had been the captain of the paddlewheel steamboat the "*DeWitt Clinton.*"

I remember music always playing...Daddy's heavy piles of 78 records...Fats Waller, Frankie Carle, Bing Crosby, Benny Goodman, Fred Astaire, the Gershwins, Rodgers and Hart and Hammerstein too...Dixieland, swing, love songs, Broadway musicals...and often a friend played the piano.

All of us dancing up and down the long front hall and around the half-empty dining room... with hats and canes, following Mummy in her top hat, doing her long-stepping dance routine...laughing, always laughing...at ourselves, at each other, and, over the years, each one of us breaking off into our own routine.

Mummy and Jojo adored the operas of Richard Wagner, and spent hours listening to them together, transported by the sensuous intensity of the music and the stories of redemption through romantic and sacred love.

Mummy's favorite and most becoming colors were turquoise, bright blues, shocking pink, and emerald green. She usually wore prints. Her cotton and silk blouses were covered with flowers and other random patterns, sometimes with ruffled necklines or sleeves. I loved her silver and gold sandals and evening pumps.

She wore old-fashioned underwear, chemises, and slips...very feminine...satin and silk and lace...soft whites...at the same time, romantic and little girlish. She always had pretty nightgowns under her quilted wrappers. I remember bed jackets, too, which we were allowed to borrow if we were sick.

She wore lots of pretend jewelry, all sizes of fake pearls. She had very little real jewelry, and what she had...some pearls, her sapphire and diamond engagement ring... was stolen from her closet one night in Florida. Neither the jewelry or the robber was ever found.

Mummy began every day with a couple of dabs of powdered rouge to her cheeks...Rouge Brunet, a bronze rose color...and red lipstick. And then, later in the day, she added powder. When we were at a restaurant, she used to pull out her compact in front of everyone at the table and, with the down feather puff, begin batting the powder onto her long nose with great gusto as she contorted her face in the mirror, sneaking a quick peek at our self-conscious reactions.

She would also embarrass me when she and Daddy came down to visit me at boarding school in Virginia, a dry state. When they took me and some of my new friends out to a restaurant, the first thing Mummy did was ask Daddy loudly to pass "Baby" to her, "Baby" being a bottle of bourbon in a brown paper bag.

And the absolute mortification, which we daughters moaned and rolled our eyes about for years, was watching her at a dance after she'd had too many drinks...sliding around the dance floor, one of her high heels parallel to the floor, her dress falling off one shoulder, lipstick smeared, hanging on to some patient partner who maneuvered her to the beat of Lester Lanin or Meyer Davis or Neal Smith.

Then, the next day, she'd ask one of us the question we dreaded most of all.

"What did I do last night? Did I do anything terrible?" There was no way to win at this game. If you evaded the question, she'd just keep pressing. If you told her what she didn't want to hear, her redheaded temperament flew into action, and you rued the words you had so foolishly uttered.

From the time I was about twenty, Mummy and I seemed to move beyond "mother-daughter" to being real friends. We loved being together. We laughed and we cried about the same things. And, occasionally, we still got irritated with each other, too.

In June of 1957, Mummy and Daddy "gave me away" to Jimmy at the loveliest wedding I've ever been to. I was twenty-three; he was twenty-two and fresh out of Yale. His Aunt Ruth was one of my mother's oldest classmates, and our parents had many mutual friends.

Jimmy and Mummy had a special bond. They saw eye to eye on most things, sharing a silent understanding. I always felt, that as close as Mummy and I were, she just might have taken his side if Jimmy and I had ever come apart at the seams.

He called her a brat, which was meant as an enormous compliment...a sixty-five year-old brat...then a seventy-two-year-old brat...and then an eighty-something-year-old brat.

In 1969, when Daddy retired, my parents bought a one-story house on the Intercoastal Waterway, on Jupiter Island in Florida.

This was a big event for the whole family; they had never done anything quite like that before. We four children all joined them for their first Thanksgiving there. We sat on the terrace under the stars. We laughed, we danced, we enjoyed good food and wine. We walked on the beach, lay in the sun, and played tennis and golf. We watched the sun setting over the waterway, silhouetting the tall sabal palms at the end of the lawn. Mummy said their heads looked like Watusis.

We thought that their spending time in Florida was a great idea. But I do remember very, very clearly Mummy taking me aside that vacation, shaking her curls and saying, "I didn't want to come here...it was your father's idea...I'd rather walk in the woods in the Adirondacks!"

Jimmy and I brought our three children and a baby-sitter down to visit for two and a half weeks every spring vacation for many, many years, beginning when Jim was eleven, Nonie was nine, and Kerry was five and a half. They joined throngs of other children swimming, bicycling, taking tennis lessons, playing bingo, going to the weekly tea dance, and ordering "Shirley Temples" and "Transfusions" and "Dusty Millers."

Gramuddy, as the children called Mummy, made everything comfortable and fun, leading her grandchildren into all sorts of games, Easter egg hunts, and make-believe. Breakfast and supper for the kids seemed to fit into her schedule so effortlessly that it wasn't until much later that I realized how cheerful and generous and uncomplaining she had been while we took over their house and their life.

After the first few years, Daddy started to get grumpy and more sarcastic. His bright blue eyes began to look sad. My children gave him a "wide berth." It seemed that after he retired he gave up, stopped using his bright mind on very much except doing The New York Times crossword puzzle in tidy little letters in ink every day, playing some bridge and golf, and reading articles and books by William F. Buckley.

Daddy's failing health began with diverticulitis. When the doctors operated, they found he had bladder cancer that had invaded his stomach. A year and a half later, he started to notice severe pains in his shoulder. He went back to the doctors, who discovered that he had lung cancer.

After several difficult hospital stays and some weeks of radiation, he came home, and, though no one was meant to say the word "cancer" to him, I knew he knew that no more could be done. I guess we all knew. At first, Mummy was most worried about what to tell their friends. But we all closed ranks around her, around them, and tried to make Daddy's remaining time bearable.

In November 1980, just a month before their fiftieth anniversary, Daddy died in his own bed, next to Mummy's bed, which she had never moved out of. With a comforting and capable nurse named Hattie taking care of Daddy, Mummy and I held on to each other in our quilted wrappers. I remember feeling awestruck, unable to help, and overwhelmed by love, all at the same time.

I held the image of his agonized expression in my mind's eye until I went down to Florida that January to open up the house for Mummy's first winter there alone. As I opened the front door with the key, I saw Daddy everywhere...blue eyes dancing, laughing, happy...no longer in pain, welcoming me in, waiting for Mummy. And that is the image of him I have been able to recall ever since.

For eight years Mummy fought her loneliness and managed her life by herself as well as she could. She told a mutual friend that she went out every night until she dropped, and then she started all over again. It was too painful to be alone for very long in her world of women run ragged by their social schedules and men doomed by their golf scores.

She fell further and further into the social soup and alcohol. And yet, amazingly, she always pulled herself together by seven thirty or eight in the morning. Her days were filled with, first, the telephone, then a little gardening, or golf, marketing, bridge games, and dinner parties. She dabbled in art class, a class on découpage, Bible class, but never really kept any of them going, usually pulled off course by a telephone call or another invitation.

Everywhere she showed up, people responded to her, laughed with her, felt better for her being there. Her health remained remarkably strong, and she looked years younger than her age.

In 1988, after a whirlwind romance, she remarried just before her eightieth birthday. On the surface she and her new husband, Gene, had a common lifestyle and some mutual friends. They had lived near each other on Long Island and in Florida for many years.

After forty-four years in the house that her mother built, Mummy moved without a backward glance into Gene's small and tidy house ten miles away. She took very few belongings with her, and, except for one small room, never added her own touch to what was to be her northern home for the next five and a half years. But she doggedly held on to her house in Florida.

On November fourth, for her eightieth birthday, her four children and all her grandchildren gave Mummy a dinner dance for about a hundred people. Gene had chosen a new dress for her, but we didn't think she looked like herself in it. It was slinky instead of the usual feminine and pretty.

The music was heavenly, and the band didn't take a break until midnight. About an hour before it ended, Gene suggested to Mummy that they go home. "Why would I want to go there?" she chided him. "There's no music there!"

And, as it turned out, there was no music there.

ON THE BRIDGE

Pages from my Journals

In the spring of 1993, Mummy had begun having sore throats that wouldn't go away. She and Gene kept it a secret until they got back down to Florida in the middle of October. There she was diagnosed with throat cancer. They and their doctor decided she would have radiation every weekday in the local hospital, so that she could spend the necessary weeks in the mild climate, traveling only a few miles from home and back. The program began in early November, and, except for a break for Christmas, lasted until the middle of January.

Throughout these weeks, their friends all said, "She's so brave, so cheerful." "They kept right up with their social schedule; she never missed a beat," and, "You'd never know anything was wrong."

At the end of the assault, her doctor congratulated her and told her she was a tough old bird. Everyone laughed. Nothing more in the way of healing care was offered. We children winced, and, amid the fifteen snowstorms that occurred that winter, took turns going down to try to help her through it.

I also spent the winter working on putting together a symposium at our local hospital, Morristown Memorial, called "Transformations in Healthcare: Reuniting Mind, Body, and Spirit."

That all began with a conversation with Bill Moyers at a Christmas party two weeks before. He asked me how things were going at the Mind/ Body Medical Institute at Morristown Memorial Hospital, an affiliate of Dr. Herbert Benson's Institute in Boston, and something I'd been the catalyst for in its beginnings in new Jersey a year and a half before. I told him of my dreams for taking the concept of wellness, healing therapies, much further into the hospital. He suggested a symposium there in the spring, and told me that if I would get the panelists, set it up, he would be the moderator. Wham!

I spent the winter upstairs in what had recently become my office on a word processor that I'd barely used yet. I began with two fingers and many names and thoughts that I'd collected from seminars and workshops that I'd attended on healing and spirituality over the past ten or fifteen years. Day by day, synchronicities would occur. Phone calls out of the blue from someone with a connection...a name and address would appear from the bottom of a pile of old papers on my desk, one I never even realized that I'd saved or had in the first place. Then letters back and forth to potential speakers who seemed appropriate, exciting. All winter long, it was as though I wasn't doing this thing myself, but it was doing me. All I had to do was hold on to the vision...easiest to do alone up in my "time capsule". Things began to happen as if in some sort of automatic gear. My computer did things that it would have taken me years to learn, ordinarily. I became clearer and braver as the days went by.

January 1994

Notes to myself while working on the symposium:

Remember...to "pray without ceasing"...to be continually connected, plugged in. Then, to be used from that place. More gets accomplished. You have no idea how big the task will be. If you did, you'd never dare to take it on. Begin, instead, from a centered place of meditation and trust, and the "road" you're to take will simply unfold in front of you, moment by moment...miracles occurring, connections being made with lightning speed right before your eyes. And so much getting accomplished, more than you know that you could ever do alone. If you can just be there with your antennae up, questions, doubts, and fears out of the way, and an overall trust to carry you through this timeless time, for however long it lasts...a week, ten days, two weeks...it will be cooked and time to let it go...before your ego rushes in to claim it! Trust and allow. Be aware. Stay out of the way.

I remember wondering for a moment if I had the courage to invite Dr. Larry Dossey to be a speaker. Well...why not! And then, he was the first to answer, left such an enthusiastic message on my answering machine. I was then, again, in Florida with Mummy. I was so thrilled when I phoned home to New Jersey and got his message that I went running out to the terrace to tell her...to tell someone...overflowing like a torrent of alphabet soup...and, of course, it was just too farfetched to begin to explain to her.

It seemed ironic given my own belief in the many and diverse ways to promote healing that there was nothing I could offer my own mother and her husband that they found acceptable, even understandable.

It was like speaking to them in a foreign language.

Life in Florida went right on. But soon everything began to go wrong. Mummy's mouth and throat were burned from the radiation. She developed pneumonia, was briefly hospitalized, and recovered.

> *"The fact that cancer and the patient's emotional life history were linked was commonly accepted in medical circles up to 1900.... Surgery focuses our attention on cancer as a local disease of a specific part of the body and not as one aspect of a total human being's functioning, which is the essence of the psychosomatic view. Radiation, coming along shortly thereafter as a therapy method, reinforced this concept of cancer as a local body problem."*
>
> *~Lawrence LeShan, M.D., "Cancer as a Turning Point"*

Tuesday, March 1994

Gene called; he's very worried as Mummy is having a lot of difficulty swallowing, and he's sure that the cancer is back. I flew down to go with them to the hospital for Mummy to have a biopsy. The results indicate not cancer, but a buildup of adhesions from the radiation on her throat.

Susie, working with a well-known herbalist, tried this winter to introduce to

Mummy some herbs, teas, soothing salves, which they felt would help. I offered a homeo-pathic remedy for soothing Mummy's throat, burned by the radiation. But they all got put up on the top of the refrigerator each time we left. My own suggestions for prayer time and for Jin Shin Jyutsu massage several times a week were dismissed, because they inter-fered with the "normal" schedule.

I can sometimes understand the polarities of life, the dark as well as the light, but right now this teaching seems impossible to accept. It's beyond our control. There's no way to know what will happen except to watch it unfold day by day, hour by hour. Quite scary, and difficult for me to trust the process.

Sunday, April 24

Early spring is so delicious here in New Jersey. The maple buds are still a haze of rosy pink against the dark purple and brown hills in the distance. An artist friend reminds me each year at this time that spring green, or "baby green," is much more appealing to paint than the "grownup green" of summer. Driving along the local roads, I see that the magnolias in people's front yards, in full, luscious bloom, were turned partially brown by a frost last night.

Dry and windy, but sunny and bright, the fine weather brings out more surprises every day now. The tulips have begun to open, the daffodils are fully out, the crabapples look like they will wait until I get back home. The wren family is back, building their new nest in the little birdhouse that hangs, blowing in the wind, on one of the crooked limbs of the old apple tree in the spring garden. Such a full and thrilling voice in such a tiny body...the Flicka von Stade of the bird world! New perfumes each day take my breath away. So soon May will arrive, and I hope to be able to spend some time like Ferdinand just being there...and here. Wait for me...I'll be home as soon as I can!

It's the day after the symposium, and I would have loved to have stayed home and basked a little while in the atmosphere of the hope of a new vision of health care. Instead, I'm in the air on Continental Flight 541 from Newark to be near poor Mummy for a while. Her swallowing mechanism has closed down, and the doctors have inserted a G-tube in her abdomen, through which a can of Ensure will be poured three times a day. She has now completely lost her ability to enjoy what was once a source of great nourishment and ritual in her life. What takes its place is simply mechanical. There seems to be nothing we can offer beyond medical interventions that is acceptable to Gene and, there-fore, to Mummy. I'm still unable to explain that there is a whole buffet of choices, other than or with Western medicine, that could help someone in her condition.

April 24, later

Susie has been down here while Mummy was in the hospital for ten days having the G-tube put in her stomach. She has been helping Mummy practice feeding herself and has tried to soothe her poor blistered mouth and face with aloe gel and herbal salves.

Now Mummy's back home with Gene and Mary, the woman who has taken care of him for many years and is now doubling as Mummy's nurse. I think Mummy was safer in the hospital. If she should choke, swallow anything, including her own saliva, by mistake, if the feeding is done wrong, if anything goes awry, there is no one careful enough, knowledgeable enough, or even kind enough to help her. It's a miracle she's made it through the winter. Their doctor says the family should be realistic and begin to accept the fact that she is going to die. Gene feels since the doctor has said nothing more can be done medically, there is nothing that anyone can offer.

> "The belief that dying patients reflect a failure of medicine and therefore of the doctor reflects the widespread twentieth-century Western superstition that 'no one dies' unless medicine has failed to save him. Death is not seen as a natural conclusion of life but rather as due to inadequacies of the medical treatment."
>
> ~Lawrence LeShan, "Cancer as a Turning Point"

But perhaps we can help. Kate will come over soon from England and will be here for two days. Then Susie and I will take turns again. Henry and his wife, Erica, will also be down at some point before Mummy and Gene return north at the end of May. I hope, while we're here, that we will be allowed to help set up a better situation, with someone else coming in to help Mummy if that's what she wants. The problem is, she will never say what she wants, and, if she does when we're not there, Gene will wear her down again until he gets his own way. Behind the effort of looking pretty and keeping up her strength, she seems traumatized, zombielike, has a haunted look.

Thursday, May 26

Mummy, Gene, and Mary returned today to Long Island. They will see their local

put Mummy in the back...blocked my way. I was told to sit in the front. They yelled, "It's going to be too bloody back there." They had to do an emergency tracheotomy. Off we went...sirens screaming...driving as fast as they could in the city midday traffic to Roosevelt Hospital. The frantic radio conversation from front to back in the ambulance indicated at first that they didn't have time to get to Roosevelt, that we would go to New York Hospital instead. Then they made a fast decision to go to Roosevelt after all.

We arrived at the emergency room entrance at Roosevelt. I jumped out of the front seat at the same time the attendants carried Mummy out onto the sidewalk. She was now unconscious and breathing better through a makeshift tube in her throat. Her suit was covered with blood. While she was taken into the ER to be cleaned up and attended to, I went to the desk with her purse to begin filling out endless forms. Henry and Gene arrived, having gone first to New York Hospital in the confusion.

Most likely in panic at what had occurred, Gene began to blurt out what had happened the night before. Apparently, Mummy had gotten up three times during the night, looking for help...at midnight, at one o'clock and at four. Each time he had led her back to her bed and then gone to his own room. The last time, she apparently fell backwards and hit her head, bleeding. He still put her back to bed. And then he'd told me the next morning that everything was all right! I don't understand this man!

Saturday, June 4

Mummy has been moved from the intensive care area to a semiprivate room. She now has not only a tube in her stomach but a tracheal tube in her throat.

Mummy can no longer speak, but she has become pretty fluent in writing notes to all of us. She keeps asking us to go over what happened on June 2.

"Why didn't someone help me?"..."Where was Mary?"..."Why didn't Gene get help?"

None of us knows the answers, so we keep asking her the same questions back. No answers.

She seems to need to go, again and again in her mind, through the horrors of June 2 in order to escape from that situation in some subconscious way. The day she woke up in Roosevelt Hospital seemed to be the first day she stepped off the merry-go-round that she'd been on for many years. She's clearer and more focused than she's been in years. As Henry said the second day he visited her in the hospital, "I will forever be grateful, no matter what happens, for this day and being able to enjoy Mummy the way she always used to be."

She even seems to have discovered some new memories. She told us today, through scribbles and grimaces, about her great aunt Lila, an unmarried artist who lived in Montana. It's the first time any of us have ever heard of her! I wonder whatever happened in Mummy's early childhood that she seems to have so few memories of her past. She remembers nothing at all of her father, who died when she was four.

Today I hosted a small Mind/Body Institute "retreat" at our house. As I was leaving to go into the city to visit Mummy, the UPS truck delivered two packages for me. One was something I had ordered. The other one was a funny-looking, weighty padded envelope. As I started to put it inside, not having time to open it, something very heavy fell out on my foot. It was a rock about a foot long with one word, "Trust," carved into it. How very timely! It turned out later to be a late birthday present from my two beloved daughters, Nonie and Kerry.

June 9, later

A CAT scan has shown a cancerous growth pressing against Mummy's windpipe, behind her voice box, blocking her food passage. There is no more that the doctors can offer. They tell us we can expect her to live a few months at best. We must help her to live out the rest of her life in peace and love.

This afternoon, Philomena Dooley arrived to visit Mummy and do some Jin Shin Jyutsu on her. I met Philomena in December 1986 in Florida when I was visiting Mummy. I had been experiencing severe headaches for about a year, and I didn't want to take drugs. However, I realized that it was time to do something, when synchronicity struck and I was introduced by a dear friend to Philomena and Jin Shin Jyutsu, an ancient self-healing art from Japan, which has been passed down by word of mouth from generation to generation and is now taught at workshops all over the world. Like acupuncture and acupressure, Jin Shin Jyutsu unblocks and balances energy flows, working on a deeper level than the body's symptoms. After only three sessions with Philomena, and continuing to do Jin Shin Jyutsu on myself, as she taught me, I was totally free from headaches within a couple of weeks and I have never had them again.

Philomena has contacted a lovely Jin Shin Jyutsu practitioner named Alexis, who will come every day to work with Mummy while she's at Roosevelt.

Friday, June 10

There has been no one doctor in charge here, but many specialists have attended to Mummy. Every day we have met someone new. All of them have efficiently given us their latest opinions and statistics about whatever body parts or organs they're dealing with, often in front of Mummy. No one will talk to us about the whole of Mummy as a human being.

Describing the modern medical outlook:

*"The viewing of the body as a conglomeration of parts, of
disease as the invasion of the body by destructive entities, of the
physician as heroic warrior; the assumption that death is evil."*

~Robert Sardello, "Facing the World with Soul"

Henry, Kate, Susie, and I had a meeting in Henry's office this afternoon to decide what to do next. In a week Mummy is due to leave Roosevelt. Susie and I offered to begin to put together a healing program at Jimmy's and my house in New Jersey to entice Mummy to come stay with us instead of going home with Gene.

Our plan would begin with Jin Shin Jyutsu for Mummy every day, because that is something she's been somewhat familiar with for a few years and now seems to love. Susie would work from Virginia with her herbalist to put together a specific plan for Mummy, using herbal teas, tinctures, and homeopathic remedies. We would start with a process of detoxification, of eliminating the toxic effects over the years of alcohol, prescription drugs, radiation, improper diet, smoking, constipation, guilt, and fears.

Because of the severity of Mummy's condition, we would need to have round the clock nursing care. I plan to find nurses through Morristown Memorial.

And, most important, we would offer her peace and quiet, prayer and beauty, and, above all, love from all her family.

There is a difference between curing and healing. Curing is scientific, acts on the physical level, "attacks" the symptoms with external agents, sometimes works, sometimes acts like a Band-Aid until some deeper work begins. Healing and curing should work hand in hand.

Healing works on the underlying cause, not just the symptom. Ideally, the symptom should be listened to, as early as possible, as a message from the body. Too often, drugs simply mask the message, silence the voice that's trying to tell us something. Healing is an individual process of removing blockages on all levels...physical, emotional, and spiritual. It works with the natural abilities of the body and the mind. The final stage in the healing process involves a letting go and may include dying. However it works, it puts us in touch with the deepest part of the self and brings us, once again, face to face with who we really are.

Henry and Kate said they didn't know much about all that, but, as there's nothing more medicine can do, they will gladly support us in bringing Mummy out to our place to give it a try. We will each offer this healing plan to Mummy at every opportunity during the few remaining days here, praying that she'll accept it.

Saturday, June 11

Today, at the well-timed suggestion of a good friend, I interviewed a nurse named Mhamuda Khan on the corner of Seventy Second Street and Madison Avenue. She was pushing a ninety-year-old man in a wheelchair. Our interview was brief, as his wife, also ninety but in better shape, rounded the corner with a scowl on her face and interrupted us. I think by then we had made an arrangement for Khan to come to New Jersey, but it was a little unclear when that would be!

Today, Mummy wrote Henry a note that said, "I'd like to go to New Jersey."

Tears of joy from all of us. I felt relieved, thrilled, and terrified all at once. After I told her how happy I was that she was coming home with us, she looked back at me and wrote, "You're taking on a heap of trouble!"

Later, I watched Mummy practicing intently with a nurse how to pull her new tracheal tube out in case of an emergency clogging or choking, and I felt squeamish and scared just watching her.

Friday, June 17

Mummy arrived at Morristown Memorial Hospital from Roosevelt by ambulance today, followed by Henry and Erica in their car. I will never forget my first sight of her there in the entry hall, sitting up on the ambulance "bed" in her ruffled pink wrapper, smiling, looking as expectant as a small, bright child on Christmas morning, one step closer to going home. However, once she was in her hospital room, I could feel the slump in her spirit. I felt bad, but I knew we needed the two days to give our own team of doctors a chance to assess the situation, and to give us time to set everything up at home.

Susie sent Mummy a Bach flower remedy that comes in a little brown bottle with a dropper, and a note saying, "This Rescue Remedy is made of flowers only, and it is a combined bouquet designed to relieve people (and animals) of worries, fears, anxieties, thus allowing calm and centeredness."

Good timing.

This morning, I met with two of Mummy's new doctors, Dr. A, the oncologist and Dr. Z, the otolaryngologist, who with our internist, Dr. R, will be on her case while she is living with us. As they reviewed her records, they both remarked that they couldn't believe everything she had been through for the past eight months, and that they were amazed she was still alive.

I explained to them that, as we had been told no more could be done medically, and we had agreed that the chemotherapy they offered was not what we chose to do, we would like to begin a healing program at our house. I also explained what that would include.

To my great relief and unbounded admiration, they told me that they thought it sounded like a good plan, that they would support us and be right there whenever we needed them. I will always be grateful to them.

*"Ultimately, it is the physician's respect for the human soul
that determines the worth of his science."*

~Norman Cousins

Saturday, June 18

Kerry drove down from Vermont, straight to Morristown Memorial, found Mummy in her room, and, after a long hug, began to do Jin Shin Jyutsu on her. Kerry will be able to stay until Tuesday, so we will blessedly be covered by a professional Jin Shin Jyutsu practitioner for the first six days. After that, for four weeks, another practitioner from Colorado Springs named Karen will come every day to lay her hands on Mummy, and sometimes on me and on Susie, when she is here. It's an amazing synchronicity. Only a couple of months ago, I was involved in orchestrating Karen's month long stay at Morristown Memorial to do Jin Shin Jyutsu. And now, she is here exactly on the day we need her!

There are no coincidences!

And so, between visits to the hospital, we began to set up the house for Mummy's arrival on Monday, by creating sacred spaces in this peaceful atmosphere, away from negative thoughts and people, preparing a place where she will feel loved and safe and taken care of and where, possibly, the alchemical process of healing might begin.

"Love is a space where freedom can be negotiated."

~Toni Morrison

This morning, Alliance Home Care arrived with a staggering amount of equipment, all covered by Medicare and all pretty horrible looking, but all necessary, it seems. Nonie's big closet became our supply station. Two cases of Jevity, an extra slanted pillow, several bottles of peroxide, saline solution, tubes of A & D Ointment, gauze, surgical tape, an extra tracheal tube. Jimmy bought an air conditioner for the window across from her bed, as well as one for Mummy's space downstairs in the dining room.

We removed one of the four-posters in Nonie's room and directed the hospital bed from Alliance up the stairs, around a couple of tricky corners, and into its place, next to the window overlooking the summer garden, the lawn beyond, and then, beyond that, the waterfall on the Black River.

Next to Mummy's bed, we set up a sturdy drafting table covered with a clean white cloth for all the tracheal care needs, the suctioning equipment, the humidifier collar, and, if needed, the oxygen.

Unpacking her various small packages and bags, we hung up Mummy's clothes, filled some of the bureau drawers, and sprinkled photographs and other little belongings around the room. Added to this, two pretty new summer cotton dresses, a lacy chemise, a healing candle made for her by a friend of Susie's, a pretty baby pillow and matching neckroll, and some herbs, all sent by thoughtful Susie from Virginia for her arrival.

We will use Kerry's room, connected by the girls' bathroom, as the nurse's station. After an enormous number of phone calls, it was heartening to find how much ready support and information there was in the community and at our hospital. Now we are equipped with notebooks full of doctors' names and numbers, nurses' agency numbers, First Aid Squad, Visiting Nurse Association, hospice, etcetera, and another notebook, sitting on Kerry's desk, is ready for all the nurses' daily notes and schedules. We are ready to begin our routine of three nurses, each on an eight-hour shift.

Today was the big day! We checked out of Morristown Memorial with Colleen, our first nurse, pushing Mummy in a wheelchair. I led the way, with all of her paraphernalia, including a portable suction machine to stick into the car's cigarette lighter if needed, to the emergency room door to meet Jimmy, waiting with his car. Seeing him there filled us both, I think, with renewed confidence.

It was so exciting to lead Mummy into our house. She hadn't been to visit us since she remarried almost six years ago. A flood of wonderful memories of past Christmases... fifteen in a row... and visits she had made with and then without Daddy ran through my mind.

Susie's brown packages have begun to arrive from Virginia: red clover, nettles, mullein, and licorice root teas, followed by faxes and instructions. Many of the faxes are for Mummy, carefully and lovingly explaining to her what all the teas and tinctures might do for her. We started with some herbal teas, slowly increasing the amounts, watching for reactions, changes. As a base to her diet, we continued to give Mummy the three cans of Jevity a day that her system had gotten used to at Roosevelt Hospital. Then, to get her plumbing working, we added some aloe gel with water to begin with. Soon we will add raw carrot juice. All of this has to be monitored so carefully because the liquids are going straight into her stomach through the G-tube.

Together, we began to plan daily programs, involving Mummy in what we are going to do together. Every evening I type up three copies...one for us, one for the day's nurses, and one for Mummy. Then I fax one to Susie for her to check. Most of the nurses seem interested in learning about the complementary therapies we are using, so I have begun to make a list with descriptions of all the different teas, the raw vegetable juices, and the homeopathic tinctures that we have chosen specifically for Mummy. I'll add to it as time goes by.

Nonie arrived from Colorado today to give us a much needed and gentle hand and to spend time with Mummy for four or five days.

I noticed tonight that the pages of my 1994 pocket diary have begun to fill up with nurses' names, three shifts a day...Nikki, Roxanne, Monica...Roxanne, Ronnie, Leslie...Alice, Nikki, Colleen...and Beth...and on and on. They are all very kind and capable caregivers, willing, sometimes even enthusiastic about wanting to understand what we are trying to do.

Friday, June 24

Mummy's days are spent mostly sitting in the dining room

in one of the

two stuffed chairs

on either side

of the couch,

which faces

out the plate

glass window

to the

summer garden.

If it isn't too hot and humid, we move with all her flowered paper bags filled with her writing paper, letters she's received, a little clock, pens, glasses, and an ever-present box of Kleenex out to the porch, which enjoys approximately the same view.

July 7
in the...

28 1994

Sometimes we stroll slowly down onto the wide wooden bridge to the two white metal basket-shaped chairs there. Sometimes I sketch Mummy while she's sitting there looking at the river.

Aug 11 199

I wonder what she's thinking about. Silence is so peaceful, so mysterious. Although we always used to have so much to talk about, laugh about, perhaps words now actually get in the way. Just when I'm wondering if she's thinking about her life or even the possibility of her death, she scribbles a note asking me a gossipy question about what someone is doing to someone else. I think of Jerzy Kosinski's "Being There" and laugh at myself.

And, yet, when Mummy looks right at me, I know she knows...a lot. But she's never talked about these subjects, and now, without a voice, she doesn't have to. Perhaps we no longer need words. Perhaps nothing important should ever be communicated except in silence.

That could certainly be one of my own lessons to learn this time around!

Sunday, June 26

I went down across the river to the studio, just to be alone and sit quietly for a while. I noticed Sogyal Rimpoche's book, "*The Tibetan Book of Living and Dying*", on the bench in front of me. I had read most of it a year and a half ago but had not had time to study it properly since then. I picked it up and opened it randomly, asking for a message. This is what I turned to:

"*Sometimes you may be tempted to preach to the dying, or to give them your own spiritual formula. Avoid this temptation absolutely, especially when you suspect that it is not what the dying person wants! No one wishes to be 'rescued' with someone else's beliefs. Remember your task is not to convert anyone to anything, but to help the person in front of you get in touch with his or her own strength, confidence, faith, and spirituality, whatever that might be.*"

Was that appropriate? I got it! So, find what Mummy does believe in and expand upon that into some kind of practice. Ahhh... *"Daily Word."* And her favorite phrase from it is "Let go, let God."

The G-tube that had been inserted in Florida fell out of Mummy's abdomen this morning. We drove to the Morristown Memorial emergency room, forty minutes away. All the way over and back, we played the *"Hello Dolly!"* CD featuring Pearl Bailey, which Mummy loves. I remember so well the night I took Mummy and Daddy to see that production on Broadway, twenty years ago, on their anniversary.

June 27 later

Today is our thirty seventh wedding anniversary, and the day Susie arrived from Virginia for ten days with her herbs and tinctures, a few more little presents, love and moral support. Tonight in the kitchen, we put on a Fred Astaire CD. Susie disappeared, came back wearing a cap of Jimmy's from the front hall closet, and carefully took Mummy in her arms to dance. Then I cut in and led her around the kitchen table a little further, in as gentle a two-step as I knew how. Mostly, it felt very special to be together, even though the dance didn't last too long.

Later this evening, Susie and I were doing Jin Shin Jyutsu on Mummy as she dozed in silence on her bed. Susie was bending over her feet, cupping her ankles with her hands; I was standing behind the hospital bed, cradling her head, holding her "fours," the two bumps at the base of her skull.

Suddenly, strong electric shocks began running down my arms into my hands. And, simultaneously, I saw Daddy standing a few feet away. I didn't want to wake Mummy up, but Susie noticed my expression. I moved my lips, my mouth, around the words "I saw Daddy!"

She nodded up and down, and mouthed back, "So did I!"

Susie has taught Mummy how to do a little tai chi, a set of standing exercises to move the energy through her body, and she practices it when she can on the bridge.

Today, Mummy asked Susie and me if she could get her hair washed. We called Tony, her hairdresser on Long Island, to ask him how to mix the color rinse she uses. Her once naturally curly, beautiful auburn hair is now varying shades of white, ash blonde, pink, or blonde, depending on the hairdresser's wrist. We got the job done, but I hope we don't have to do that again too soon.

Susie showed me the proper way to steep the bulk teas she brought with her in a mason jar, using a straw strainer. We began by alternating mullein and licorice root teas, Susie explaining to Mummy and the nurses what they were for.

Wednesday, June 29

Today we brewed Essiac tea for the first time, using the bulk brand called Flor-Essence by Flora from the health food store which had been recommended by most of the people we've asked. Curiously, but not so surprisingly, both Susie and I had been receiving information on Essiac all winter and spring.

> *In 1922, through one of her patients, a Canadian nurse, named Rene Caisse, learned of an herbal tea used by the Ojibway indians which combined sheep sorrel, burdock root, slippery elm, and Turkey rhubarb. Over the years that she used this recipe, she "maintained that Essiac caused regression in some cancerous tumors, the total destruction of others, prolonged life in most cases and, in virtually every case, significantly diminished the pain and suffering of cancer patients."*
>
> ~ *Gary L. Glum,*
> *Calling of An Angel: The True Story of Rene Caisse and... Essiac*

Susie made the first batch, stirring the brown bubbling mixture slowly, mysteriously, like a witch's brew in a caldron, and then pouring it into sterilized mason jars to be stored in the dark in the refrigerator.

When we offered it to Mummy tonight for the first time, she refused to take it unless we did, so we each had a cup, and then, ceremoniously, poured her brew slowly, slowly through the tube into her stomach. What kind of alchemy will happen in this vessel?

Thursday, June 30

Jimmy is in Vermont with Kerry and Terry for a couple of days. Tonight, Mummy, Susie, and I were having supper in the kitchen with one of the nurses, Roxanne. Suddenly, we felt the house encircled by a wild, tornado-like storm. A large branch of the old yellowwood tree outside the kitchen was twisted off its trunk, missing the house by inches. The lights went out, meaning that Mummy's machines upstairs were out also. Strange weather in a strange, otherworldly time.

Two kind, strong neighbors came to help us and hooked up a generator next to the house, snaking a large red cord up through Mummy's window to plug her machines into. Throughout the chaos, our interior bubble with Mummy, our port in the storm, remained calm, in the world but not of it.

Friday, July 1

The suctioning of the tube in Mummy's throat makes such a harsh and horrid noise, but it does do the trick. It's hard to comprehend the endless mucus she keeps having to deal with. The nurses' notes continually mention "coughing thick secretions...thick white mucus." I don't know how she keeps going sometimes, never complaining, just methodically filling Kleenex after Kleenex, trying not to waste them. She always carries the box of Kleenex, the little flowered paper bags filled with her daily needs. They all go with her...upstairs, downstairs, outside, inside.

Sometimes when the inner tracheal tube is cleaned, a plug of mucus that looks like Carter's glue comes out. I realize, again and again, the danger we're dealing with.

Mummy had always slept like a log until this winter. I can hardly imagine the terror she must feel about the possibility of choking. We asked the doctor for a very mild sleeping prescription and were assured that Dalmane would be the best. Unfortunately, it seemed to put Mummy on another planet until 2:00 P. M. the next day. I threw out the pills in disgust, and we began, instead, to give her drops of tincture of valerian root, and later passion flower, in half a cup of water. They worked just as well, but with no after effects at all.

Saturday, July 2

Philomena stopped by unexpectedly this evening, spent time with Mummy. She read her pulses to see which energy flows needed attention, then did some Jin Shin Jyutsu on her, and, after that, joined us for supper. She makes us feel surer of where we are.

July 2, later

Nightly trips in the dark with Susie, after we've tucked Mummy in bed and said good night, take us to the bridge to sit in the two round-backed metal chairs, to watch the fireflies in the meadows and in the trees on either side of the river. This feels like suspended time, no time. We sip our own Essiac in small blue and white pottery mugs and chat a little, but, mostly, we become absorbed in the silence and the magic and gratitude.

Monday, July 4

It's the Fourth of July. Susie, Mummy, and I sat in the dining room on the sofa and two chairs, sketching an arrangement of flowers I'd collected from the garden.

Mummy's flower arrangements were always original, spritely, even bratty, full of her energy and personality. But now, she doesn't really have the interest in making one, though she gave it a try today.

We had chosen a red, white, and blue...and yellow... blouse from Mummy's closet that looked somewhat celebratory for the occasion. But there will be no fireworks this year.

Gramuddy
7/4/94

in dining room

Mummy went upstairs for an afternoon nap in bed with the humidifier collar on. She needs to do this most days now. We try to schedule an hour-long Jin Shin Jyutsu session afterwards, so she doesn't have to make any extra trips up and down stairs.

Susie left today for Virginia. She sent me a fax when she got home, which said in part, "Feeling overwhelmed to be home...Hope you're O.K. Everything's so perfect for Mummy there. It's just great. Remember, I'd be glad to take her here (if we get to that point)."

Together, we grope our way further into foreign territory.

We took Mummy to see Dr. Z, her throat doctor, today. On the drive over to his office, she began pointing to the car radio and with her index fingers dancing up and down, asking me to play *"Hello Dolly!"* again.

When we got home, I gave her the book *"Like Water for Chocolate"*. She says she likes it. She refuses to read *"Embraced by the Light"*.

This is definitely one of the strangest times in my life...so far. Mummy with us now with tubes in her throat and in her stomach, unable, for the last three months, to eat normally, and unable to speak or swallow for the past five weeks. But, thank God for twentieth-century technology when we need it. We would never have had a chance to have Mummy here without it.

I feel like I'm spiraling downward, free-falling into a vortex...nothing to hold on to, no edges, no walls, no boundaries, no time, no expectations. It's where I'm meant to be...here with her. I've parked my "normal" life without a backward glance, except for an occasional phone call and break to come up for air. The plans I'd looked forward to...visiting and painting out west this summer...evaporated faster than I could erase them from my pocket diary. The bubble I'm living in with Mummy...with the round-the-clock nurses, the daily Jin Shin Jyutsu sessions, the equipment from Alliance Health Care, the "diet," Essiac, herbal teas, fresh vegetables to be juiced, daily schedules to be printed up...feels like a strangely protected place, full of love, and occasional apprehension.

Mummy is extraordinary in her acceptance, her trust, her cheerfulness. I don't know how it will turn out for her; I know I don't need to know. The only thing that fills me with dread now is the possibility of her going back to Gene, to a situation that could, and almost did, kill her.

At breakfast this morning with Jimmy and the Sunday papers, I asked him how

Mummy could possibly be so accepting, such a good sport. She's like a little girl but

seems to understand everything on some nonverbal level. Isn't it queer?

To lose her ability to speak in order to, maybe, remember

things in the silence. He says he thinks she understands it all.

I just stopped in to see her at 10:00 A. M. and found her sitting, in her pale yellow short cotton wrapper, on the edge of her bed, facing the window that looks out to the waterfall, feet dangling over the edge of the bed in her gold leather slippers, with Susie's tall, thick, blue candle lit, reading Daily Word. Her expression is one of total peace with a little merriment added. To be able to see her like this is worth everything.

Mummy looks so different than the way she looked this winter and spring in Florida when she seemed confused, medicated, brainwashed, anything but peaceful. Now, she's off the treadmill, and in touch with a part of herself that had, perhaps, been lost or overshadowed.

Every day, she studies the day's printed plan...what's in each feeding, who's coming to visit, how many drops of valerian root at night, what time someone's coming to give her Jin Shin Jyutsu...and, together, we wade into depths unknown.

Medically, of course, we've been told the prognosis is hopeless. And yet, things seem to be happening, changing. Her body seems to be beginning to fight for itself. Has she made a choice yet, whether to stay or leave? Perhaps she's at a point of trying to decide.

Squeezing fresh carrot juice...spinach, cucumber, celery... making herbal tea infusions from the little marked brown paper bags that come from Susie in Virginia, brewing the Essiac recipe late at night, working out the schedules and nurses, spending time with Mummy, making trips to the health food store, running errands. If I ever feel tired and down, I think of her spirit and forget my own small problems. What an enormous teaching this all is, and, most of all, she is.

Two of the most important self-disciplines for me to keep up now if I'm going to be here in the right way for Mummy are my daily meditation and some exercise, both of which, all too often, get lost in the rituals of each day. Just when we think we don't have time for them is when we need these things the most! Most of the time I notice, just being here with Mummy in this strange and altered state, that our life together has simply become one long, unending prayer.

Thursday, July 14
Bastille Day

Rumble...rumble...Thunder getting closer...the air feels electric, smells funny... everything outside is an eerie green. Listen with fox ears...I hear the waterfall...I hear the birds making a hurry hurry chirping noise, a little bit like they do when they sense the great horned owl approaching...and then...more thunder. It's getting dark. I'm sitting on the couch out on the terrace, under its roof. The garden has lit up against the eerie green. All the colors seem more luminous. The coreopsis is a bright yellow gold; platycodon, violet blue; white nicotiana; cosmos. Pink, peach, white lilies; lavender-pink phlox just put in, alchemilla's acid green leaves, orange-peach daylilies; and, at the far end of the garden, the statue of Nathan Hale, liberated from the cellar when we moved in here twenty years ago, silver-bronze today, in this light, looking upriver like a scout watching for the storm.

Everything feels infused with spirit this summer...the intense beauty and clarity of the garden, the environs, the movement of the birds, the great blue heron, and Mummy's peaceful expression. It feels as though we are living slightly out of time, suspended beyond time.

I can't really tell how Mummy's doing. She looks remarkably well, but she's having trouble breathing, particularly on very humid days. One voice inside me says she's been detoxing up until a few days ago, and now her body's trying to heal itself, that perhaps there's a chance. The medical world says...what we don't want to hear.

A flash of lightning. Mummy's inside; she hates thunderstorms. I like being out here, alone just for now.

Our days have been running quite smoothly. I'm keeping centered, pretty calm. This weekend will be a test. The old leak in the girls' bathroom really acted up with all the use Mummy and the nurses are giving it. It seems the pipes in the sink are the problem. Water has been pouring through the light fixture in the little annex to the kitchen that we're using for juicing, storing, etcetera. Yesterday, the carpenter hacked away the ceiling, then the plumbers came and did their thing, and now the place is a shambles!

Saturday, July 16

Henry and Erica came out for the weekend. We had a happy dinner in the kitchen with Mummy tonight.

Monday, July 18

Karen left to go back to Colorado, and now Joan M, a practitioner and friend who lives in our area, will begin Jin Shin Jyutsu on Mummy as many days a week as she can. Her gentle demeanor and strong hands have already given Mummy confidence. We often play the tape called *Rosa Mystica* by the harpist and music thanatologist, Therese Schroeder-Sheker while we do Jin Shin Jyutsu to help Mummy let go of anything she might be holding on to.

Overload, panic yesterday. Keeping everything up, keeping up the house…literally, as it seems to be falling apart…the many extra houseguests, lunch guests, meals, unmade beds, conversations…has suddenly gotten the best of me. Our "healing atmosphere" feels like a claustrophobic prison. Out of here! I got in the car and drove to the mall. I bought some sheets and curtains on sale, half of which I left there and had to go back for, plus some lipstick, face cream, and a trio of tee shirts for the price of one which I really didn't need.

I look old and tired, even after Jin Shin Jyutsu; my skin is too wrinkled, my hair is too short. I need exercise, but I can't seem to make myself do it. The summer feels heavy today. So do I.

The not knowing is wearing. Is Mummy staying on here? Is she going back to Gene? Is she still, in the midst of her bravery, playing the same old games, not saying what she means? Will she ever speak her own voice? And does that have anything to do with the blockage in her throat?

We never know, from week to week, with each visit by Gene, how long she will stay. She will never say, but, instead, buys time in small increments each time he is here, using Jin Shin Jyutsu or a nurse or something else as a reason to stay. I suspect she will just keep doing this for as long as she can without actually telling him she isn't coming back.

This afternoon, Mummy said she didn't want to go to the doctor tomorrow. Nor did she want to have the X ray of her chest and shoulder area, as she feels that Joan M is finding the source of the problem through Jin Shin Jyutsu, and the pain has gone. That's good news. I called Dr Z and he left me the out-of-town number where he'll be for the weekend...just in case. Bless him!

Drawing on br--.

Jimmy and I went to the movies tonight...hot dogs and popcorn and Mountain Dew...a great escape from health food, and it tasted deliciously bad. We saw Forrest Gump. I sobbed and sobbed, overflowing tears into a sodden lump of Kleenex...throughout the movie, out to the car, and all the way home. Something about man's inhumanities...and kindnesses...to each other really undoes me. Might also be the dam bursting after seven weeks of uninterrupted Gramuddy.

Saturday, July 23

I wrote Mummy a letter today:

"Dearest Mummy,

I don't know how to tell you how much I love you, and love having you here with us. To think that seven weeks ago you were an inch or a minute away from dying. I look at you now, so beautiful, so peaceful, so full of light, and I can't believe so many terrible things have happened to you...and now, so many blessings, so many things to be thankful for. A second chance in which to appreciate and look back on your life, and to really understand who you are and why you're here on earth.

It's clear to me that you are here to bring light into many, many lives. Everyone you come in contact with...your friends, the nurses, the hairdressers, children, people of all ages and walks of life...all see it, are touched by you.

Let your light so shine…and don't ever stand in its way!

I heard a wonderful analogy once at a funeral. The minister was talking about each person's life being like a unique patchwork quilt. The owner could only see the backside of the quilt while she was here…all the knots, the mistakes, the broken threads that went into it. Not until she left this plane could she and everyone else see the magnificence of the front side of her quilt.

Well, you, having been given this new lease on life, can begin to see the front side of your quilt as well as the reverse…through the eyes of all the people who are writing you and asking after you, and all of us who are taking care of you.

All that any of us want in return is for you to understand and acknowledge who you are and how very much you mean to us.

I love you,   Joanie"

Of course she never mentioned my letter, but neither did she throw it away.

Saturday, July 23, 10:45 P.M.

Whew! Khan has arrived, after all. I feel the great weight that has been on my shoulders being lightened. I interviewed this remarkable nurse about six weeks ago in New York while Mummy was there, and then she disappeared. It turned out that her husband had quite unexpectedly died in a hospital-induced accident in South Carolina. She must have been shattered; no wonder we didn't hear from her.

And now, here she is, coming into our lives to take care of Mummy. I hope we can take care of her as well.

We welcomed her into our lives. She was stunned at her first sight of Mummy. "She looks so well, so young...she's beautiful!"

And, you know, when I kissed Mummy good night a little while ago, the light was pouring out of her eyes, her face radiating love, and trust, and, yes, appreciation. She really is beautiful.

All the nurses have been dedicated and caring, each in her own way. But having one person round the clock all the time will be much easier, more relaxed. And if Mummy does get better and better, Khan can go anywhere she wants with her, or they can just stay right here.

Sunday, July 24

With Khan having settled in and taken so much over, I've gotten out the easel and begun to paint watercolors again, outside, next to the studio garden...daylilies, echinacea, bee balm...and the peach-and wheat-colored field beyond. Sitting here in the black swivel chair in the studio, I am surrounded by new beginnings...large watercolors with added pastel...nothing finished, still plenty of possibility.

There is a shifting of gears that needs to happen before I can begin to paint something, or someone. It is a moving from looking to seeing...from exterior to interior...a moving inside that's necessary between the artist and her subject. Sometimes it takes days; sometimes it happens in an instant. But, no matter how many years I've painted, every time I stop for a while or move to a new scene, I always need to go through this initiation process.

To truly see in painting is to allow time to stand still, to become intimate with each subject…to see the holiness in everything, in everyone…to slow down…to take time… to be completely present. It's the way I feel with Mummy now; the way we should all be with one another. Here and now, that's easy to do during this unhurried and languid summer.

Tuesday, July 26

Susie arrived yesterday for another eight-day stay. She and I, having breakfast, are back on the number-one subject. Is Mummy turning a corner? Is she getting ready to die? What is the confused face? What is the sad face? The peaceful face? Does she want to tell us something?

Henry has firmly said to Mummy that she must tell Gene what her plans are. That's not her way. Perhaps we should just leave it as it is. She seems to know what she's doing.

Khan and I talked about the possibility of Mummy's death and, in what manner, from her own experience, she felt that it could happen. She mentioned the same things the other nurses and doctors have described as possibilities…choking, hemorrhaging…I told her we understood, and that we wouldn't go to extraordinary means to stop it…that if that was to be, we only wanted to try to make it peaceful, make her as comfortable as

Wednesday, July 27

I stopped in to see Mummy on my way down to breakfast this morning. She was already sitting up, and Khan was changing her G-tube dressing. Apparently she had a good night, and she looked pleased. I told her I'd been thinking that it would be a good idea to tell the "throat thing" that she doesn't need it anymore...that, if she will speak her own voice, be firm about everything, tell it to go away, she will get better. Khan nodded in agreement. Mummy looked at me, wanting to believe, not negating the idea...child-like, curious.

Friday, July 29

A special day. First of all, the weather, after weeks and weeks of intense heat, and a lot of rain lately, was spectacular. One of those high-ceilinged, sunny, clear days, when the shadows are black, the darks are so dark, the lights so bright. A day you wish from the beginning you could save for another time.

I began another large watercolor by the studio garden, or, rather, practically in it. The white phlox standing out against and above the rail fence, a contrast to the cinnamon and peach and citron field behind. An echinacea with a butterfly on it...bee balm, cosmos. I now have about seven or eight paintings in progress in the studio. I call that the "buddy system." Oh, it feels like such a release to be back into it. I can't wait to start another one tomorrow morning.

At 1:30, I went up to the kitchen, made egg salad sandwiches on pita bread for Susie, Khan, and myself, and brought our lunch down to the bridge to eat, picnic style.

Mummy, Susie, and Khan had been sitting in the three wrought-iron chairs there for at least an hour.

Mummy was attempting to draw with a black felt-tipped pen.

Khan was doing her needlepoint and, in between stitches, looking dreamily into

the river; I can't imagine what she must be going through herself,

having just lost her husband.

Without words, we were each lost in our own thoughts
and yet bound together in the heightened state of
love and beauty that pervades our days.

A little later, Susie and I drove to the Town Farm in Oldwick to pick up fresh peaches, corn, and tomatoes...the best part of any New Jersey summer...We took our dinner into the dining room to sit next to Mummy while we listened to Cole Porter.

Khan said this morning, "Imagine if she recovers. It could help millions of people."

It has crossed my mind a few times, too, but I try not to get too attached to the idea or the outcome. Day by day...by day...by day.

Tuesday, August 2

Susie left this morning about ten thirty, leaving Mummy instructions, tai chi exercises, and feeding suggestions for Khan and for me. Susie does like things her way, and shakes her head in disgust at differing opinions. It's all right, though. We all have our roles, and I'm so glad to be working with her. The good vibes between us far outweigh the annoyances.

Mummy is obsessed with her sleep. Khan says all old people are. She must, understandably, be worrying about her lungs filling up, or choking, or something hideous like that. I'm sure she must've overheard one of the doctors or nurses in New York talking about "aspirating." These were some of the same comments being bandied about in Florida, come to think of it. She's probably terrified to go to sleep, subconsciously.

August 2, 10:30 P.M.

Late in the afternoon, Mummy and I were sitting in the dining room, she in her usual stuffed chair, I on the couch next to her. I began to talk to her about how important I felt it was for her to consciously spend time during the day, and night, when she was awake, with God. I told her that all of us on her team could take care of the food, the Jin Shin Jyutsu, the Essiac, the healing atmosphere for her, but that it was very important that she work on prayer and its healing.

I explained to her how comforting it was to me to put myself purposefully in the presence of God. I suggested that it would be helpful to bring her mind down slowly from her head, down into her middle, then to repeat a phrase over and over, like "Let go, let God," while breathing in and out. "Be still and know the peace that passeth all understanding."

We did this for a while. Later, in the library, she wrote me a note asking me when I found time to spend with God. I was so happy that she'd really been thinking about it, and I told her it was sometimes hard, but that after a while, it became such a lovely place to be in that I wanted to be there more often. And, after a while, I said, it's kind of fun to bring God right into the garden or the kitchen or wherever you happen to be.

Tonight, when I went into her room, she asked me if we could do it again together.

Wednesday, August 3, 7:45 A.M.

Lately, I always wake up tired. My head hurts from the humidity. The locusts screeching in the trees make the heat feel even more oppressive. There's mildew on our ceilings, the house needs painting. I need to call the painters, set up a date. I think of Mummy and what she must wake up to. I think, perhaps, I'd just pull the covers over my head and stay there. Her spirit amazes me.

Tonight, Jimmy came home and turned out all the lights so that Mummy could see the great horned owl outside on the lawn. Finally, she really saw him through the binoculars, about a hundred yards away, and she was so pleased with herself. He's so cute with her, so real, such fun, just the right blend of teasing, kindness, showing her things. He's always loved her. We ate dinner with her, then read. We talked, she wrote notes...very comfortable.

At 10:15 she went upstairs with Khan, and I went in to see her about half an hour later. She pointed at the healing candle, the one Susie had had made for her. I helped her light it and we put it on the night table. Then we held hands, and did our meditation.

"Close your eyes. Feel the presence of God...all around you...around your head, touching your shoulders...loving you, taking care of you, keeping you safe.

Now, while we hold hands, just stay in the silence, be with God, and we'll say together, slowly...silently...over and over, 'Let go, let God'...until I let go of your hands...'Let go, let God.' "

According to Khan, Mummy coughed up something at 5:00 A.M. that looked like "a piece of flesh, somewhat bloody." We're a little hopeful that this could be the beginning of the Essiac breaking up the "thing" in the throat. When it works, that's apparently what happens.

Jimmy and I are going to the Cape for twenty-four hours on Sunday to see Nonie and her group, there for two weeks from Colorado. Henry and Erica will be here in New Jersey while we're gone.

Saturday, August 6

I came home with the groceries about 7:00 P.M. With Mummy and Khan, I watched two and then three hot-air balloons hissing and floating toward us from across the driveway. For three days now, Mummy's breathing has been labored, in her chest area, her lungs. It's been a different noise, dry, but heavy and difficult.

Tonight while I was cooking and she was next door in the dining room, she began gasping...then panicky breathing...a scary and scared expression in her eyes. Khan and I took her upstairs and got her into her bed with the humidifier collar on. Khan took her blood pressure, which was very high, 200 over 110. I thought she was about to leave us there for a while, but, eventually, everything calmed down. I just kept saying to her, "Let go, let God, like we've been doing," and telling her not to be scared, that she was being protected. It seemed to calm her, but, mostly, I felt she was not really there. Maybe we won't go to the Cape tomorrow.

Cape Cod, Monday, August 8

At 5:00 A.M., the phone calls began from New Jersey. It was Henry. He told me that Mummy was having a nightmare of a night. Henry, Erica, young Jim, and Annie had had a nice dinner...Mummy with them...in the kitchen. Everyone went to bed around 11:00 P.M. At 3:00 A.M., she got up, Khan with her, then passed out in the bathroom. Khan rushed to get Henry, in the guest room next door, to help her. Together, they carried her back to her bed. Her breathing had become a real struggle. This continued for a long time. Her blood pressure was going haywire. She almost died twice. Henry said he wished he knew how to help her because she was struggling so. I told him to hold her and say with her, "Let go, let God"...that we'd been practicing that a lot...

Later, during another phone call, when things had calmed down, he said at the end, "Oh, you know that thing you told me to do?...It really seemed to help."

By the time Jimmy and I got home at 6:30 or 7:00 this evening, the war stories and the camaraderie were in full swing. It filled me with joy to see how close they'd all become, after never having spent that much time together. Henry told me after dinner what a good guy he thought Jim was, how helpful Annie had been. Khan raved about Henry, he about her. It wouldn't have happened if we'd been there.

Tuesday, August 9

Except for three uneventful trips to the bathroom, Mummy slept through the entire night last night, having also slept through all of yesterday.

This morning, as Henry got ready to leave, I saw Mummy's eyes fill with tears.

August 9, later

Dr. A came by for a visit. When he asked Mummy to tell him where it hurt, what felt different, what was on her mind, she made an attempt, twice, to make him laugh, avoiding having to answer the questions. I guess some things will never change.

Mummy had a small amount of fresh blood in her tracheal tube at three o'clock this morning.

After shopping and then cooking for the many meals needed for the relatives coming through this weekend, I was able to take time to paint one sketch of Mummy down by the bridge in my sketchbook. Painting is a meditation.

Jim arrived at the bridge to visit his "Grammy," and sat with her while I washed my hair. He is her oldest grandchild. They've always made each other laugh, but now he has a hard time seeing her like this, with the tubes in her throat and stomach, surrounded by machines. Still, he comes as often as he can to play gin rummy with her, setting up a portable CD to bring her "her kind" of music...Cole Porter, Ella Fitzgerald, Pavarotti, Gershwin...to entertain her.

Around 6:30 P.M., I baked bread to get myself out of my head. Jimmy's away for a few days, so I ate dinner sitting with Mummy on the couch in the dining room, waiting for Kate to arrive from London for six days.

Mummy's breathing is not good. We began an antibiotic today as prescribed by Dr. A. We're also trying to balance doses of Lasix for her swelling.

Kate arrived about 9:00 P.M., in time for late supper and catch-up. Mummy was very anxious, so we all went to bed around 9:45, after saying prayers in the silence with her candle. I think it makes her happy; maybe it just makes me happy.

At 2:00 A.M. Khan came to get me. Mummy's breathing desperately again. Khan gave her Lasix earlier, and has led Mummy to the bathroom seven times during the night, once more while I'm there. Taking her blood pressure, mopping her feverish forehead, we gently encourage her. Can she make it again through one of these crises? I don't want her to suffer. I ask Khan about beginning morphine by making a sign of a shot on my arm. She asks if the prescription is from Dr. A; she knows it is. Then she gives Mummy a small dose, pricking herself by accident with the needle first. She tells me it depresses the nervous system. I know. I watched its effects on Daddy fourteen years ago. Mummy gets groggy; the panic leaves her open right eye. At 3:00, Khan tells me to go to bed. I linger after I blow out the candle, saying silently, "Thy will be done, Thy will be done," and then go back to my room.

I feel she's going to go. Bless you, dear, adorable Mummy. I only wish, before you go, that I could understand your private thoughts, your deeper feelings. I know you're timid, and sensi-tive, too. I can see that in your little attempts to paint. Your handwriting's not timid, though.

These nights must be so scary for her. Her breathing is so labored, like trying to suck air through a wet straw. Her whole chest heaves in a sucking in, and then, a very shallow exhale. Her eyes are always open, steadily holding my own, asking, trusting... at first, full of fear; but then, after the prayers...and sometimes a little morphine...the terror subsides, and she closes her eyes.

August 12, 10:45 P.M.

Kate's family arrived from London this evening. They are asleep down the road in Jimmy's sister's cottage. Mummy's asleep for now. I just left her. We did our "surrounded by the Presence of God, protecting you, keeping you safe from harm," then repeated "Let go, let God." Peace came over her face again.

Kate mentioned before she left for the night that she'd had the oddest feeling of waiting all day. I've had that feeling too, for the first time, in the aftermath of last Saturday and Sunday nights. For me, the shift has been that any hopes that I've held on to have gently been let go of. Could the feeling be contagious? Does Mummy feel it, too? She wrote the strangest note tonight, and she seemed insistent that she meant just what it said: "Why am I here only tonight?"

Is Khan going to wake me up tonight, or is it going to be peaceful? God bless Mummy, and Khan too. And all of us.

Saturday, August 13

I think Mummy knows. A part of her seems clearly to know her time is running out. I feel a close, unspoken connection with that part of her…through her eyes, through gestures, through what she's not saying. An intense conversation without words. It feels as though we are in somewhat of an altered state. Is this the beginning of the transition? Are we at a new way station?

I called Susie to tell her that Dr. A reads the latest blood tests as inconclusive, but as cancer; and also to tell her that the pulse readings by our Jin Shin Jyutsu people indicate the beginning of the end, trying to warn her that it might happen.

Three more relatives want to come spend time with Mummy tomorrow. The hardest part of hosting this whole operation has not been taking care of Mummy, but my needing to feel that I'm keeping everyone else satisfied…caught between trying to keep a peaceful, quiet atmosphere and allowing everyone to spend time with Mummy in their own way. Everyone is so sure of what they believe and feel, and that, of course, includes me. I'm not proud of the way I react sometimes. They all have as much right to see her as I do. There are many lessons for all of us. I remember my oldest friend, Lili, telling me that her own mother's illness and subsequent death brought everyone in her family so close.

The four of us are very close to begin with…all very different, of course, and yet, all Babcocks, each with a unique blend of genes, karmic homework, experiences, and astrological blueprints. Naturally, there are different points of view about how Mummy should be taken care of…a few clashes, a few differences of opinion. But all four of us and our spouses have offered and given our love, our advice, our expertise. And Mummy, subtly and typically, has allowed each one of us to take care of her and tell her what to do.

Everything worked out fine. Henry and Erica brought fabulous leftovers from a dinner they had eaten the night before, to feed the six or seven people who were here...a welcome change from my own cooking. There was nonstop conversation from one o'clock on. Mummy seemed fine, seemed to enjoy it all.

I can't tell if it's my own anxiety, the sudden shift out of the peacefulness I've worked so hard to protect, or a result of three bad nights. I must let go and trust. I guess the hardest part for me is not reacting to, taking personally, the little criticisms and the second-guessing dropped here and there...like, "We should have had Lasix starting Sunday night."

"Suffering is reactivity," I know. Not reacting is easy to do when one comes in for a short stay, a day and a night here. Maybe I'm overly sensitive now. Maybe? Yes, terribly. I think I'm worn out, but I don't want to leave until it's over. I feel like I'm crumbling, cracking, being prickly, sensitive, emotional. I need a dramatic change after this is all over. There'll be time for that later. I suppose it's human, but I feel guilty that, because we've had a couple of times of thinking we were losing Mummy, my mind fast-forwards to a funeral, or thinks about getting away, or wishes that, if this is the end, it would hurry up.

And, then, I see her, lying in her bed when we say our prayers, looking trustingly at me, and I come back to the present and never want to let her go.

I had a nice time sketching Mummy on the bridge this morning before Kate and her family arrived. She stays in one position now, partially, I think, to give me a chance to finish my sketches. I'm glad she didn't ask to see the two I did today, as, when I looked at them tonight, I was struck by her deterioration from the earlier ones in the sketchbook. She still has the cutest face, but her ankles are now enormous and swollen. Khan says it's the fluid.

August

Lasix and an antibiotic now every morning; echinacea once or twice a day.

Aug 14

August 14, 10:45 P.M.

The heat wave has returned… broiling, boiling, sweating hot. Our house smells of mildew. Thank God for the air conditioners Jimmy bought for Mummy's room and her downstairs "headquarters" in the dining room. I kissed Mummy good night about twenty minutes ago, after our prayers, et cetera. She looked at me with knowing eyes, with love and appreciation and a childlike expression that's so appealing. Facing another night would be so hard, I should think, with the possibility of having another scare, but she moves on, always, and looks as trusting as ever. It amazes me. Maybe she'll be around a little longer than everyone thinks now.

Monday, August 15, 7:45 A.M.

It looks like a beautiful, clear, and cooler day today under the still drawn window shades. I hope it will clear the air…particularly in my own head. Jimmy and I had a "pillow talk" last night. He told me that they're all just trying to help me.

"They all have a right to be here. Imagine yourself in their shoes and wanting to get into the act."

He tells me I've done a fantastic job, that Mummy was almost dead, and that what we've done is a miracle. I guess that's all I really needed to hear.

In the beginning, and until very recently, I've been able to take these two and a half months day by day, through each crisis, each change, each difficulty, and to concentrate my energies on Mummy. It was wearing, but, oddly, quite wonderful. Now, with this latest shift suggesting that the end may be in sight, with everyone moving in on this peaceful, separate world, the rest of the world floods in to join the still waters, and I am caught in a whirlpool of emotions. Change is inevitable, the only thing we can ever count on. My own role has become clouded. Before, trusting in the not knowing felt sure and close to the source. Now I must remember how to do that again.

I picked up a little book of prayers by Henri Nouwen called "Circles of Love", which had made its way, somehow, to the top of the pile on my bedside table. I opened it randomly to a page titled "Prayer of Little Faith."

"Prayer of petition is supposedly more egocentric. The prayer of little faith is where you hold fast to the concrete of the present situation in order to win a certain security. It is filled with wishes which beg for immediate fulfillment. This prayer has a Santa Claus naiveté which wants to satisfy specific desires. When the prayer is not heard, that is, when you don't get the present you wanted, there is disappointment, even hard feelings and bitterness. The man of little prayer prays a prayer that is carefully reckoned, even stingy, and which is upset by every risk. There is no danger of despair and no chance for hope."

I guess I fell right into that one, didn't I?

I took a chunk of the day off today and played some tennis, did pool exercises, and laughed with my buddy Arlene. I've managed to get out of myself now a little more, and my nerves are calmer. Exercise helps me to let go. It's hardest to remember this when one actually needs it the most.

Wednesday, August 17

Mummy's upstairs now having her Jin Shin Jyutsu session with Joan M. I'm sitting in the chaise longue outside the dining room, taking a little time out to survey my garden. It's been so very beautiful this summer...probably just for Mummy. Thank you, all you little devas and fairies, for delighting me and Mummy every day this summer with your continual arrays of blooms and colors and artistic arrangement. And for flower arrangements, and painting subjects, too.

The Bonica roses, down by the dam and on either side of the bridge, are in the midst of a profuse second explosion. The daylilies, up in this garden, across the river, and mostly in the "survival of the fittest" garden by the studio were the mainstay of July. Now, except for a few late bloomers, they're gone, leaving a lot more green than we're used to. The platycodons are still producing their lavender-blue balloons, but they, too, are getting skimpy. The white phlox has gone to seed up here and has lost its freshness down in the studio bed, where it did make its way into a couple of watercolors earlier. The nepeta, scabiosa, coreopsis, echinacea, malva, and the sweet faithful rose, Little White Pet, are still making an effort. The midsized cosmos that we grew from seed are pretty fillers; a peach-pink zinnia adds a touch here and there; a bit of impatiens, some annual blue salvia; the white nicotianas are not even trying. I must remember not to plant them again next year.

Now the dahlias and the Japanese anemones have begun, I know that summer is on the wane. I think Mummy is, too. I feel a restlessness in her and, therefore, in me. A dull sense of panic, of wanting to bolt...wanting to cry... spreads through me. I don't want to leave her and, yet, now and then, I just have to get in the car and go...marketing, mail, somewhere. Letters go unanswered, paintings unfinished. For over two and a half months, I've given up everything else in my life but Mummy. I know I'll always be grateful that I did. I think what's happened to Khan has also happened to me. We really believed she was going to make it until Sunday...Monday...I still don't know. The moment those hopes faded, my mind began to fast-forward to what might happen, and, mostly, when. I've had to call it back from its wanderings again and again.

Will she be here this fall? Will she die next week? Can I plan a painting trip? Where will she be for Christmas?

Poor Erica wants an answer about whether or not to move her son Ian's wedding date forward or backward from September 17. I can't help her.

Saturday, August 20

A state of Grace...gentle and protected time...often silent and unhurried, not going anywhere. Being completely present in every moment, whether it's in pain or pleasure, sorrow or joy, laughter or tears. Having to live each day as though there were no future, as there is no way to know what that will be...no way to know how long she will be with us, here in New Jersey or anywhere. Praying without ceasing.

To one who waits
all things reveal themselves
so long as you have the courage
not to deny in the darkness
what you have seen in the light.

~Coventry Patmore

Monday, August 22

I told Mummy tonight that I was going to go to the Cape for a week, and asked if that was OK with her. She nodded and smiled "yes," and patted my hand. I asked her if she'd be here when I got back, and she nodded yes again. So, I'll drive to the Cape tomorrow and Susie will move up here from Virginia while I'm away. I'm leaving extensive lists, schedules, plans, doctors' numbers, et cetera. Seems pretty airtight.

Henry and Erica are prepared to move in for a second week after Susie leaves if all goes well. I feel I need to explain to them what we've been doing...the program...that it has taken a lot more work than just calling the doctors and putting Mummy on drugs. We need to watch every day, change the schedule, the intake of fluids, food.

The three doctors appreciate what we're doing, say that they are amazed at how well Mummy seems. She's nutritionally way above average. Kahn says that, of the hundreds of cancer patients she has cared for, Mummy is the only one who dosen't smell of the disease. As far as we know, she is in no pain, has enjoyed peace of mind, and is all there in the head except for the after effects of drugs administered a couple of times recently.

We wouldn't want to quit this regime now. It's important for anyone coming in to be with her to honor this approach, to listen and watch, and then to make careful and gentle decisions.

Looking at the officious list of doctors, maps, telephone numbers, schedules that I'm leaving, I feel a little sick...of myself. I know I have to give up control, and allow the others to take over. Let go, let God.

I wish that one of us could have a conversation with Mummy, and ask her if she's thought about her funeral, her favorite hymns, if she knows where she'd like to be buried. These seem like natural questions to me, but I know they're not to her. There's never been a door open to anything like that so far, and I think that's not going to change, so I probably won't ask. And, once again, as it's always been, she will have caused everyone else to make the decisions and take care of the details.

On my long drive up Route 95 to the Cape today, I kept thinking of that dear little figure doing tai chi on the bridge, of sketching her, of wanting to do more...thought about our two trips to the emergency room and two trips to the doctor's office, and how, each time on the drive over and back, she would point to my CD player on the panel and with her hands and expressions make dancing motions until I'd turn on "*Hello Dolly!*", and, no matter how scared or worried she might have been, she'd keep time to the music and smile. We all pretended we were just having a good time. Actually, we kind of were.

Then I thought about the little black dots still on her neck from the radiation last fall, the tube in her stomach, the tracheal tube in her throat, the mass and fluid in her chest, the unending mucus she's had to deal with for so many months...none of which she has complained about...and I saw her, after she goes, free from all those hindrances, free, and smiling, and full of light, and beautiful, and funny, and dancing. And then I knew how much I will miss her, and, yet, still be close to her, as we are so close, so linked. I hope she'll send some of her spirit, her sense of fun, her light touch to me when she's moved on. I sure could use it.

Anyway, I wept and wept as I drove, and began the process of letting down. I need the break, but I know how much I'm going to miss her and, particularly, our little nightly prayers. Jimmy will fly up to meet me tomorrow night. There will be no houseguests. It will be so nice to be just us. He's been so great about Mummy, and is now urging me to stay up here for two weeks.

Tai Chi on briny

What a strange time this is. Just strange. The world is in chaos; people are having such difficulties. Each one of us is being hit over the head however and wherever it hurts most, where the lessons are to be learned, where there's the most amount of work to be done, the most change needed. The Universe is telling us to wake up. Pay attention. Let go of what no longer works. Pluto in Scorpio. It seems to be "checkout time" for so many, too.

Conversations seem to hang in midair, heavy with meaning on many levels. I watch people and see their own struggles, big and small, written all over their faces, changing the expression in their eyes. They move slower, seem more deliberate. Perhaps it's only from this new place I'm looking. My own world has certainly slowed down, has even, seemingly, stopped for eight weeks.

Cape Cod, Monday, August 29

Henry and Erica will be taking Susie's place in two days. From everyone's accounts, it sounds like Mummy's doing as well as can be expected. Our internist will be on call all week, so the situation seems well covered. I've agreed with Jimmy to spend a second week up here.

Susie was very upset the other day on her watch, when she discovered that Gene, there for his weekly visit, had taken Mummy off in Jimmy's car without telling anyone, and without any precautions. Now, a week later, I realize I really am on vacation, as I begin laughing out loud at the idea of a couple of old fossils, wanting to have a little fun, escaping in the "getaway car." Turns out it might even have been Mummy who suggested it!

Mummy's apparently better, out of the woods again, but weaker. The swelling in her hands and feet is the worst problem now. They've upped the dosage of Lasix. She's not going down to the bridge much anymore. She falls asleep often, but is peaceful, although they feel she's ebbing away. I hope they'll all have some fun together...time for a little lightening up. Seems just right that Henry and Erica are there this week with Mummy to see, firsthand, what's going on, and to be a part of it all. I'll be going home in five days...precious time. Now that I've taken a break, a part of me dreads the return, but a part of me wants to be with Mummy, too.

This cool weather heralds the familiar feeling of the end of summer. I feel a lonely pit in my stomach, an old memory of not having done my summer reading. I never did, and, though I've surely more than made it up in time spent reading over the years, the feeling will probably haunt me every early September for the rest of my life. This time of year, too, is always a reflective time.

It's a balancing act now...balancing Mummy's diet, medications, herbs, and tinctures, balancing Susie's approach, Henry's thinking, Kate's input from London, including Michael's medical questions, Gene's visits, the doctors' prescriptions, and on and on. I feel like a trapeze artist, wondering what's happened to the safety net below.

Tuesday, September 6

Home again, after a five-and-a-half-hour drive with Jimmy and Kerry. We arrived here around 3:00 P.M. Dear Erica had waited for us, before going home to Long Island.

I found Mummy sitting, nodding off, in her chair in the dining room. I was startled to see that she had on an unfamiliar dark green wool sweater over her very familiar pink and white cotton dress, the one Susie bought her in July. I was suddenly aware of the shift in seasons here. She got up. Her hands and her ankles were so swollen that the skin was stretched, shiny and tight, over the almost unrecognizably puffy parts of her. Her stomach was bloated. Her color, waxen, gray and pale under the rouge. Her hair has grown longer in the two weeks I've been gone. She looked at me, a little apprehensively. I stepped forward with my arms outstretched and, putting them around her, held her silently for several minutes, rocking the two of us together. Everyone else gave me knowing looks, but what, really, does anyone know?

Kerry and I did Jin Shin Jyutsu on her for about forty minutes, and then again, briefly when Mummy went up to bed. The swelling in her hands came down slightly, but her ankles, under the covers, still feel enormous. Her breathing doesn't sound good, despite the oxygen, the Mucomyst, and the Prevental. It certainly looks like she's not going to last long, but she's surprised us before.

Wednesday, September 7

Dr. R was here at 6:00 P.M., and painted us the following picture: Peripheral edema in hands and feet, etcetera. Probably caused by low protein count. She's getting plenty of nutrition, but her body is no longer able to process it. Therefore, the fluid goes into the tissue of her arms, legs, feet, and hands, with some leakage.

It is suggested that we increase the Lasix to two times a day.

Her right lung has either fully collapsed or partially so. It could also be pneumonia, or a little of each. Suggest Cipro-500 mg 2x a day. Due to one lung not working sufficiently, her oxygen count is very low...75 to 80. Suggest increasing oxygen to 3 1/2 liters from 2 1/2 or 3.

Thursday, September 8

The new medicine for her right lung seems to have helped, as Mummy had a good night last night. Her edema is still bad; her skin looks like it might burst. Her color is odd...yellow to gray, despite the rouge that always goes on. Her eyes are bulging out, particularly the right one...and still, she looks beautiful to me. That sweet, sweet face...still making funny expressions, still lighting up, but not quite as often now.

> *"Generally by the time you are Real, most of your hair has been loved off and your eyes drop out and you get loose in the joints and very shabby...but these things don't matter at all, because, once you are Real, you can't be ugly, except to people who don't understand."*
>
> *~Margery Williams, "The Velveteen Rabbit"*

Two friends of Mummy happened to be in New Jersey and said they would like to "come see Kath." There were plenty of times, earlier in the summer, that I would've loved to have had her friends see her here, and see how well she looked. But now, I feel the need to protect her. Each week all summer, after his visit here to see Mummy, Gene has reported nothing but bad news to their friends. Jimmy and I agreed that Mummy should not be on display now.

This afternoon Mummy and I sat outside the dining room,

next to the garden...Mummy bundled up in her

blue and green mohair shawl on the chaise longue,

a throw over her feet.

I sat close by in a metal chair,

deep into my watercolors and sketchbook,

painting her.

She sat there, very still, very dreamy, as though she had

slipped into another time and place.

I kept sketching her,

beginning another page, and then another,

delighted to have this uninterrupted time myself.

She turned to look at me just as I finished three or four sketches, so I moved over to sit on the edge of her seat, by her legs. Holding her hands, and then, holding her in my arms, I began to talk to her about the subject she'd never wanted to discuss. I felt, at last, that I had her silent permission. How to begin?

I began: "One of us is going to die before the other...and I think, perhaps, it might be you."

She smiled, and patted my hand. I went on to tell her how much I loved her, how much we loved having her here, how much I would miss her physical being, but how I knew that she would always be with me, with all of us. I told her that I wished that, after she'd gone, she would leave me some of her spirit, her lightheartedness and sense of fun, because I needed it. She smiled, nodded yes, hugged me, and kept silently saying "thank you" about everything I told her. She looked radiant, and, later, beckoned me to hold her again, all without words. I think sometimes they do get in the way. Twice later, after a small shot of morphine, she tried to tell me something. I felt bad that I couldn't read her lips. I gave her a pad and paper, but she's unable to write legibly anymore. Something doesn't connect. I made light of it and told her that it was all right...she just doesn't need her writing skills anymore, and we laughed.

She told me, mouthing the words, that she was ready to go,
that she wasn't scared.

I looked at her face, at her mouth, her expressions,
even in this condition, and thought about how I'd miss her.
I cried as I hugged her and told her, as I felt my tears touch
the side of her face, that I was crying because
I loved her so much.

"Truly, it is in the darkness that one finds the light; so, when we are in sorrow, then the light is nearest of all to us."

~Meister Eckhart

Mummy's breathing wasn't good tonight. Khan gave her morphine again at 9:00 P.M. I wish that she could go peacefully in her sleep. I hope it will be soon, before any more physical nightmares happen. So far, I don't believe she's in pain or is suffering that much. It seems as though she's in some kind of twilight zone, and getting ready to go.

It was only about 65 degrees out today, though perfectly beautiful. But Mummy was too weak to come downstairs. Gene arrived around eleven o'clock; Henry arrived shortly after. We sat together in the spring garden off the south end of the house, where it had been too hot to sit all summer, huddled in the sun, out of the wind, and discussed the possibilities of Mummy's funeral. We all agreed that she would be buried next to Daddy.

All the earth has a new magic look to it. These clear, bright September days make me long to get out and paint landscapes, take off. And yet, I want to be here, nowhere else. As the end gets nearer, I want to be with my Mummy every moment. My mother, my child, my beloved. We've been so intimately close in the peace and the pain of this summer, knowing so many things together. I feel no remorse, no regret. The summer was a gift to me, as well as a gift from all of us to her. The moments of grace and joy far outweighed the times of terror and suffering. And now, after our silent communion, understanding even more, sharing this new and sacred place she's allowed me to enter, this womblike space of birth and life and death all in one. It will be difficult, and yet a relief, to let her go.

Tonight she had on a pair of flannel pajamas I'd not seen before...white with tiny dark blue flowers. She looked adorable. She tried to tell me something. I can't remember her words, her silent mouthings... something about not being able to go. Was she talking about dying or not being able to go to the bathroom? She looked wide awake, a little anxious. So we surrounded ourselves in the now familiar Presence of God and love. Her eyes closed...then opened...then closed... then half opened...then closed again. I stayed there on the side of her bed with my own eyes closed for a few moments, holding her hands. Then I gently took my hands away and got up to leave. She opened her eyes, waved her hand, told me to go to bed. I promised to come back if she needed me. Khan promised also, as she always does, to come get me during the night, if necessary. Before I left, I thanked Mummy for being my mother, and she said silently,

"My luck."

> *"Is it possible to prepare for our death with the same atten-*
> *tiveness that our parents had in preparing for our birth? Can we*
> *wait for our death as for a friend who wants to welcome us*
> *home?*
>
> ~*Henri Nouwen, "Our Greatest Gift:*
> *A Meditation on Dying and Caring"*

I'm sitting on one of the three metal chairs on the bridge alone this time. Mummy won't be down here again, I know. I feel overwhelmed with sadness. Today I cleared away, cleaned up, the sitting area in the dining room that has been her downstairs "headquarters"...old letters, writing paper, pens, a stuffed dog, two big boxes of old albums and photographs that Henry left here, books she's been given, some she's read, a book of bad jokes, some children's drawings, a CD player that I've now put back in my studio, a padded towel on top of the upholstered chair she sat in. I put away the letters, the glasses, her address book, so much stuff, things that are so much her, that she will never use again.

Erica's son Ian's wedding is to be in Darien this weekend. Will Mummy die before or after that? All the family will be going, of course, and stopping here on the way. I realize that the Divine plan is orchestrating itself better than any we could have put together, and it is now building up to a crescendo. I must spend ample time in meditation. It's the only way I know to stay centered while the chaos goes on around me. The calm before the storm. Give me strength, Oh God.

I think, as I watch the river from the bridge, flowing away beneath me, of allowing everything...all of my thoughts, any worries at all...to blend into the ribbon of light winding its way down and around two turns, and, then disappearing behind the far bank of trees. Oh, to understand that life, like the river, is always changing, forever flowing...through rocks, through drought, through storm...just flowing on. So hard if you're not a river!

Tonight is peaceful. Mummy's edema has improved, her hands are back to near normal. She even succeeded in writing again, a little more legibly, a few letters missing here and there, but at least they were letters. She's wide awake now, lucid, often lost in thought. I wonder what that is, and where. There's no worry or fear on her face. She looks quiet, peaceful, surrounded and filled with love.

Monday, September 12

We went to bed around 10:30 tonight, after an anguishing time of watching Mummy in a wheelchair upstairs, completely out of it, sleeping, head lolling to one side, drugged by the morphine sulfate I had taken responsibility, with the internist, for putting her on. I had thought it would ease her pain, lessen her suffering. Khan kept reminding me of how much clearer she was before it took effect. It worked wonderfully for a couple of days but seems to have had the cumulative effect of putting her into a stupor, something we've worked so hard all summer to avoid. Her bodily functions are beginning to go. Her right lung has collapsed, a systemic breakdown causing the fluids to seep out through all the pores of her body. Her breathing is labored and shallow. I've tried so hard to keep ahead of her so she won't have to suffer, and now I've jumped the gun. I only wanted to help her go more easily, and, instead, I feel like a murderess. O God, help...please bring her back to lucidity.

Tuesday, September 13, 3:00 P.M.

Mummy came out of her morphine haze around 1:00 P.M. today. Thank God! We have her back. Susie's been grilling me from Virginia on why we were giving it to her in the first place. It seemed to affect her so well for the first day and a half, but then, whammo! the wheels came off. I'm just glad it's over. Now we'll go back to having Khan give her morphine by injection only when her breathing gets scary. She seems to know best.

I just lugged home eight bags of groceries for the coming tidal wave, plus rubbing alcohol, peroxide, A & D Ointment, and Depends. As I left the Super X with two big bags of Depends, I turned to the checkout girls, who seemed to find my situation amusing, and said, "The time between needing Pampers and Kotex, and then Kotex and Depends isn't very long, so enjoy it! " They nodded their heads in horror and agreement.

Suddenly this summer seems to have been very, very long. I look back through three months' pages of my pocket diary and all I see are nurses' schedules, Gene's weekly visits, Susie's three seven-to-ten-day visits, Henry's, Kate's, the grandchildren's visits, two trips to the emergency room, and two visits to the doctor. There were also several visits to Hannah's garden to pick up fresh eggs, but mostly because Mummy so enjoyed spending time with Teo, the gardener. And there were so many family dinners with various combinations of us all, Mummy sitting at the head of the table in what was once her own Queen Anne wing chair, just listening, smiling, enjoying her family, until she could no longer be there.

Even the dark and difficult times have been rich ones, parts of the whole. It has never been my way to focus on those times, but I'm very much aware of the dark, particularly when I'm in the middle of it. Reminding myself that pain and joy are inseparable is the only way I know to navigate the uncharted waters we're in right now.

"At the bottom of the abyss comes the voice of salvation. The black moment is the moment when the real message of transformation is going to come. At the darkest moment comes the light."

~Joseph Campbell

I spent the evening from 7:30 on at my friend Sinikka's house with some special friends...my sangha...who've been praying for Mummy, for me, all spring and summer.

I brought my sketchbook of her, as I have reached the last page and wanted to share it with them. Now, through the sketches, they know a little more about her. They were so loving and appreciative, and I appreciated them more than they will ever know.

Kate and Michael arrived from London about 8:00 P.M. last night; Nonie came earlier from Colorado. The first thing Mummy asked Nonie was, "Are you going to get married?" Some things never change! Annie and Jim came by to see Mummy, and then the seven of us trooped down to have dinner around the dining room table, leaving her upstairs. Everyone is here on their way to Ian's wedding. The timing is amazing.

Khan banged on my door at 2:30 A.M. I knew this time it was time.

As I had on other middle-of-the-night calls, I put on my pink and white wrapper, brushed my teeth, brushed my hair, then felt my way in the dark across the bottom of our bed to the door so as not to wake Jimmy. I groped my way into the hall, across the landing, and into Mummy's, room, to her side. She was sitting in the wheelchair.

Sucking hard for air, perspiring, she still managed to recognize me, looked steadily at me. The oxygen was on, making its low, groaning noise; the humidifier collar was placed over the tracheal tube in her throat. Khan continued to suction the tube, and sometimes her mouth. With each pull of the suctioning, I winced inside, hardly able to bear having these things done to her anymore. Khan asked me to help Mummy stand up so that we could change her Depends and put her on her bed. She allowed us to do this as she has allowed everything we've done to her, like a dutiful child.

We pushed the wheelchair as close as we could to the bed, then hoisted Mummy up and over onto it. I pushed the up button to raise her head. We put the pillows comfortably behind her. Every time Khan left her alone for a moment, I began to say the prayers we've been saying together all summer long, repeating at the end," Let go, let God." It seemed to relax her. She closed her eyes, then opened them again as she concentrated on trying to breathe. Her breathing began, every once in a while, to stop...and then, to start again. Her color paled; her tracheal tube kept falling out. I held on to her hands, which, like her legs, were slimy with sweat and A & D Ointment. Her breathing began to stop more frequently, became fainter. Khan kept coming at her with the suction tube. I said no...no more, though I knew she was only trying to make it easier.

Finally, no more breathing. We took off the breathing collar together. Khan turned off the machines...suction, vaporizer, oxygen. Silence... Peace...

I felt a tremendous release from Mummy, through me. Thank God, it's over. Even in death, she looked like she was just sleeping peacefully, more peacefully than she has in a long, long time...with no attachments. Khan removed the tracheal tube from her throat, revealing the open wound. I pulled the covers up to just under her chin to cover the deep, dark hole in her neck. No more.

I longed to stay with her for a while, alone with her, her spirit, wherever she was. I sat beside her in the predawn quiet for what seemed like a very long time.

"Be still, and know the Peace that passeth all understanding."

At about 4:30, I woke up Nonie in the guest room next door. It was the first time she'd seen someone she knew who had died. She told me that when she had gone in to see Mummy upstairs just before going to bed at 10:30, she had suddenly looked up toward the left corner of the room by the ceiling with a surprised expression. Nonie asked if someone had come to see her. Mummy nodded yes. Nonie asked her if it was a man...No...Was it a woman? No....And then she blushed and turned away. I'm glad to know someone had come. I wonder who it was.

September 17, 5:00 P.M.

The great blue heron Mummy had loved watching all summer just flew by and up, way, way up to the top of a vine-covered tree across the river. Simultaneously, six Canadian geese flew low, right by me, calling their sad September call of moving on. Now, the heron is sailing through the air, downriver. The garden is still blooming, the final stages. From full bloom to death; from death to new bloom... as changing as the river, and as unending, too. The white miniature roses off the end of the terrace where we sat so often look like five altar pieces. The sky is overcast; it's about to rain. I'm too tired to walk, and now the rain allows me just to sit quietly for a little while longer.

I look from this vantage point at several of the places that Mummy sat or walked. Of course, where I sit is right where she sat as I painted her not so long ago, the last four watercolors in my sketchbook. The bridge where she attempted to paint, where she followed Susie's tai chi instructions, where she threw the tennis ball in the river for our labrador, Cecily. It must have been an effort just to do those simple things. She always made it look enjoyable, sometimes even fun. Her attitude set the tone for us all. Her peace of mind transformed not only herself but everything and everyone around her.

The hospital bed and all the equipment have been taken away, and Mummy's room looks disrupted, at best. I put the room back the way it used to be, and created an altar on the bedside table for Mummy. First, some fresh flowers from the garden in a little cranberry glass vase. Then I found September's Daily Word which had been lost for the past few days under a pile of books, and opened it to September 17...and there it was..."Let go, let God!"... Mummy's favorite! I left it open to that page next to the lamp.

The little fairy doll that we had brought into Roosevelt Hospital to cheer Mummy up when she first arrived there, was  still pinned to the lampshade. I lit Susie's candle, and will keep it going every night until after her funeral on Thursday on Long Island.

Sunday, September 18

Jimmy and I drove home last night from Ian's wedding in Connecticut. So many emotions in such a short period of time. Toward the end of the reception, I had paused on the dance floor for just a moment and noticed with delight that the only people still dancing were Babcocks...of all ages. Mummy would have been proud of us.

Today, Susie and Kate came to spend a night with us on their way to Long Island. This evening we three sisters spent time together in Mummy's room, sitting by candle-light on the floor by the makeshift alter, sharing memories, prayers, and silence...and finally holding hands and saying together, "Let go, let God."

The last three months have been an amazing time for me. Deep into somewhere I've never been before. Anguish and joy. The Grace of God. Most of all, great love, a silent teaching from Mummy...a teaching without words...about courage and trust and smiling brown eyes. About spirit unbroken...faith unspoken. About peace of mind and the transcendence of pain. About love and intimacy. About blending the visible and the invisible, and losing track of boundaries. About mystery.

I miss her terribly, miss her physical presence, our conversations of old, and the easy connection through our eyes when she could no longer speak. I'm happy she's free from the impairments of illness and of old age. Funny, her character, her cheerfulness, her countenance kept us from really seeing all of the struggles she must have been going through until her spirit left them behind in a large pile of medical equipment and useless belongings.

On this rainy and interior day, as I write letters about her, I feel her presence so strongly. Just now, I can feel her sending her love to me. Suddenly, I see and feel her standing there, just a couple of yards in front of me by the window, looking younger, and yet every age and no age. She's all in white, radiating light, smiling her smile, and love is pouring out of her eyes onto me, covering me. I feel my heart pounding, a ringing in my ears. I find it hard to breathe. It is overwhelming.

I know now she'll always be with me, and, though it makes me sad to think I can't be with her in person anymore, I know I'll never not be with her again.

Nothing seems at all real to me here these days, including my life. I'm not in a hurry to pick up where I left off many months ago, not ready to pick up the telephone and reconnect with the other world. Everything has changed; nothing is as it used to be. Who am I, really? What am I doing here? What am I to do now...and for the rest of my life? A terrible loneliness comes over me. I'm not ready to go back to "normal," whatever that may be. For now, I'd rather just keep writing letters and remembering, staying here in her presence, and in the Presence of God. Before I forget.

AFTER

I am sitting on our terrace in New Jersey, nestled into the faded blue cushions, on the same wicker chaise longue that Mummy spent so much time on that summer three years ago...a summer that changed my life forever. It seems like so long ago...and like only a moment ago.

I watch the play of light on the pale pink and blue and white colors of the June garden, and on the waterfall in the distance. Much nearer, I look at my bare feet and giggle to myself because they look so much like Mummy's.

On the ground next to me are the beat up old pair of pink-trimmed white Belgian shoes which she wore almost every day she was here with us that summer, and which I almost threw away after she left us.

I never wanted to own Belgian shoes...too snooty, too expensive, too everything I didn't want to be identified with. And, here I am, the Cinderella who fit into all four pairs she left behind! They are comfortable, and as Susie said when I first tried them on, "It's OK, they look cool with blue jeans."

Since Mummy's death, I've had to come face to face with my own inevitable death someday, and to begin to focus on how I choose to spend the rest of my life.

For the first few months after Mummy left, I mindlessly allowed my head and my pocket diary to fill with the same things that had seemed so important or necessary before. But over and over again, an inner voice kept repeating, "Been there; done that."

So many things had lost their meaning. Life felt flat, and my energy was running out. There was no turning back from the threshold I stood on now. To choose to walk "in the valley of the shadow of death" with someone you love is to begin a process of initiation that will change life forever.

That spring, I began to get "messages" to put a book together from all the writings and watercolors and mementos I'd kept from that summer before with Mummy. Then one day, I treated myself to a massage. While I was lying on my stomach on the therapist's table with my face in the hole, I suddenly "saw" all the pages of the book...from my journals and lists and sketchbook...fall like shuffling cards into a pile on the floor below...with the angel of Mummy I'd painted for our Christmas card on top as the cover.

So I began what would be a journey into the dark for the next three years, with the writing of the book as my vehicle.

Quite suddenly, I found myself clicked into a different space, slightly removed from my normal awareness, and teetering on the edge of a vast and dark abyss. I watched everything that went on from what seemed a safe enough distance...continually "changing my glasses"... adjusting to the view.

With an odd detachment and trust, I watched my life, each day, each event, go by like a movie...frame by frame...month by month...for almost two years. Somehow I managed to keep up the appearances and appointments of our "normal" life as needed.

The breaking up...or down...of what was no longer working in my life felt like a series of little deaths. The word shatterings kept running through my mind.

One by one, I began to focus on, and then let go of, old disappointments, worn-out daydreams, even some people who were no longer appropriate to what my life was now about.

Day by day, I began to loosen the grip of my own will, allowing the stripping away to occur, and feeling the recurring pain of the inevitable mourning that followed each change.

"Thy will be done."

I wondered so often, during my dark night, if 1 was going to die. Had I done everything here that I was meant to do? I was exhausted and I was ready, if that was what was meant to be. I wasn't afraid of death. I was, I suppose, afraid of life continuing as it was...a dead end.

I could sense a Master Hand at work, playing out a plan that had been orchestrated slightly beyond my reach.

> *I said to my soul, be still, and let the dark come upon you*
> *Which shall be the darkness of God."*
>
> - T. S. Eliot, "East Coker"

The only way that I knew to make my way through that dark and Plutonian labyrinth was to hold on to the presence of God, to spend every moment I could in "God's time," just as I had learned to do with Mummy that final summer. And to keep saying to myself, over and over again, "Be still and know"...in the silence, in solitude, even in the midst of conversation.

The pain was great when the strings were being
tuned, my master!
Begin your music, and let me forget the pain,
Let me feel in beauty what you had in your mind
through those dark pitiless days."

- Rabindranath Tagore

Finally, this spring, the heavy clouds began to evaporate. A new sense of joy coupled with a sweet sadness infused my being. I felt newly born.

Soon afterwards, our first grandchild, Audrey Slade Brady, was born on the evening of my own sixty-third birthday.

All day, as we waited, I felt Mummy's presence, as though she was waiting, too, involved in some way. I kept seeing her hands, her fingers, tying ribbons.

Half an hour after Audrey's birth, we met her in her mother Annie's arms, her father, Jim, standing dazed and proud beside them. She simply looked very familiar. It was like looking in a mirror, seeing one's reflection in a clear, still pool.

I knew immediately that she was the gift of joy that Mummy had promised to send me after she died. My heart exploded open.

As I watched her expressions, I thought about the trauma of her birth, and then about the pain and suffering she'll have to go through during her lifetime here.

But mostly, when I looked into that little face, I saw pure, unhampered spirit that hadn't yet forgotten where she'd come from.

Sometimes now, when I push Audrey in her carriage, I watch her looking overhead at the passing trees. She seems to go somewhere else, to see something I cannot see. Her look of total bliss reminds me instantly of Mummy's expression during some of her final days. A Divine connection at the beginning and end of life.

We have work to do together, and love and stories...and fairies...to share, not to mention a birthday every year!

There are moments...alone in the evening, in the silence...in the garden... that I know. I know everything that I need to know. I am loved with an overwhelming love. And I feel brand new.

"Inside this new love, die.

Your way begins on the other side.

Become the sky,

Take an axe to the prison wall.

Escape.

Walk out like someone suddenly born to

color.

Do it now.

You're covered with thick cloud.

Slide out the side. Die,

and be quiet. Quietness is the surest sign

That you've died.

Your old life was a frantic running

From silence.

The speechless full moon

Comes out now."

- Rumi

"Rumi...These Branching Moments"

translated by John Moyne and Coleman Barks